The Narrow Passage

THE NARROW PASSAGE

Plato, Foucault, and the Possibility
of Political Philosophy

GLENN ELLMERS

NEW YORK · LONDON

First American edition published in 2023 by Encounter Books, an activity of Encounter for Culture and Education, Inc., a nonprofit, tax-exempt corporation.
Encounter Books website address: www.encounterbooks.com

Manufactured in the United States and printed on acid-free paper. The paper used in this publication meets the minimum requirements of ANSI/NISO Z39.48—1992 (R 1997) (*Permanence of Paper*).

FIRST AMERICAN EDITION

LIBRARY OF CONGRESS CATALOGING-IN-PUBLICATION DATA IS AVAILABLE

Copyright information for this title can be found at the Library of Congress under the following ISBN 9781641773430 and PCN 2023938562.

1 2 3 4 5 6 7 8 9   20 23

Contents

Introduction

And when the LORD *thy God shall deliver them before thee; thou shalt smite them, and utterly destroy them; thou shalt make no covenant with them, nor shew mercy unto them....*

But thus shall ye deal with them; ye shall destroy their altars, and break down their images, and cut down their groves, and burn their graven images with fire.

Deuteronomy 7

If philosophy is evidently required by the human situation, grave consequences necessarily follow for our everyday conduct as well as for society.

Leo Strauss[1]

YOU ARE BEING MANIPULATED. But you already know that.

To take one small example, the psychologists employed by the social media companies figured out years ago that giving and receiving "likes" on Facebook and Twitter will stimulate a small dose of dopamine – the "feel good" chemical in your brain.[2] If it seems like the Internet is addictive, that's not your imagination. Other ways of influencing our choices and behavior are subtler and more indirect, though it can be difficult to see who or what is behind the manipulation.

More generally, Americans are lied to on a daily basis – by corporate advertisers, medical hucksters and spiritual charlatans, the sensationalist media, and of course the authorities in government. This has become normal, even expected.[3] Again, it is not always immediately clear what purpose all these lies serve or who is orchestrating them. I do not mean to promote any conspiracy theories of either the Right or the Left. In fact, some of the most influential academics of the 20th century developed a convincing framework decades ago that accurately describes the current environment of official deception. We will examine below one of the most insightful of these writers, Michel Foucault.

The best way to think through these cultural and technological issues, and the questions they raise, is on the level of politics. Human beings are social creatures. From the smallest details to the biggest questions, our opinions and habits are framed by the political community in which we live. We shape our laws, and they shape us.

But something has gone terribly wrong with the American political community. It has been a long time since the people of the United States fully exercised their sovereign authority to choose the officials in government whose primary job is, or is supposed to be, to protect the people's natural rights according to the Constitution. Our political community has become something different. America, our "regime," has become post-constitutional. Yet it is not entirely clear what this post-constitutional arrangement is, how it operates, who is in charge, or how to fix it. (A later chapter will examine what has been called the bureaucratic "hollow state.")

In April of 2022, the author and social psychologist Jonathan Haidt wrote in *The Atlantic*:

> The story of Babel is the best metaphor I have found for what happened to America in the 2010s, and for the frac-

tured country we now inhabit. Something went terribly wrong, very suddenly. We are disoriented, unable to speak the same language or recognize the same truth. We are cut off from one another and from the past.

It's been clear for quite a while now that red America and blue America are becoming like two different countries claiming the same territory, with two different versions of the Constitution, economics, and American history. But Babel is not a story about tribalism; it's a story about the fragmentation of everything. It's about the shattering of all that had seemed solid, the scattering of people who had been a community. It's a metaphor for what is happening not only between red and blue, but within the left and within the right, as well as within universities, companies, professional associations, museums, and even families.

Haidt's essay makes a number of thoughtful observations about the sources of these discontents. But his analysis – which leads him to think this fragmentation happened "very suddenly" – does not dig much below the surface. While some things have changed very rapidly, it seems likely that the deeper crisis facing American society is not sudden at all, but has been unfolding for a long time. Nor is it limited to the United States. From Brazil to Canada, Australia to Western Europe, even to some degree in Iran and China, we see rising tensions in response to similar issues. Haidt rightly argues that the effects of social media are part of the problem. But in some ways Facebook and Twitter merely amplify the more fundamental controversies: suspicion and resentment over COVID policies; bitter conflicts regarding immigration, race, and cultural identity; the seemingly unstoppable power of woke ideology in popular culture, sports, business, academia, and the media – all connected to a deepening antagonism between populists and global elites.

One reason the current political situation seems so strange and confusing is that western civilization may be going through a massive transition. Many contradictions and tensions that have been building for a long time – over decades, or even centuries – may be reaching a breaking point.

In particular, this book will explore how two incompatible strands of modern philosophy are relentlessly diverging. On the one hand, the scientific and bureaucratic experts in the corporate world and government are enlightened cosmopolitans, who rely on empirical disciplines such as engineering, sociology, epidemiology, criminology, and economic modeling to justify their rational administration of society. Because this specialized wisdom is purported to be objectively rational, the rule of expert administrators is thought to transcend the old-fashioned need for the consent of the governed. This question of knowledge and freedom will be a recurring theme of the book.

At the same time, however, our elites are increasingly in thrall to an ideology of ethnic separatism and various dogmas of postmodernism. Nihilistic absurdities once confined to university seminars are now becoming authoritative in law, business, and even the military. Fields of knowledge and intellectual disciplines that had been considered objectively true are now dismissed as hegemonic, white, male constructs. Thus the same ruling class that defends its authority on the basis of scientific expertise also insists on identity-based truth, such as Afrocentric calculus and feminist chemistry. There would seem to be some concerns with the idea that competence in flying a commercial airplane, for example, should be determined by the goal of overturning white privilege. But even more worrisome is the erosion of political and moral principles once considered neutral and essential for any free society. Due process, rules of evidence, and especially freedom of speech are no longer seen as impartial goods to be defended even for one's opponents. Many political leaders and prominent intellectuals seem to be increasingly in favor of the doctrine of the old Soviet criminal code, which denied that "class enemies" had any rights. In place of due process, the Party would decide who is guilty on the basis of "revolutionary justice."

There are irresolvable contradictions, which can't be papered over forever, between objective science and postmodern ideology. Acknowledging these contradictions can be psychologically painful and politically confusing, especially for the activist Left. This might help explain some of the disproportionate anger, the arbitrarily shifting pronouncements and priorities, the readiness to pounce on ever-changing "enemies of the day." At the risk of seeming overly academic, we can refer to this irreconcilable conflict between scientific bureaucracy and woke irrationality as the tension between Hegel and Nietzsche. The premise of this book is that we urgently need to revisit these abstruse thinkers, as well as some others, in order to think through the theoretical tangles of our political and cultural situation. At the moment, it seems neither the Right nor the Left has much to say about key questions of political philosophy.

Blue America is highly politicized and focused on doctrinal purity, yet seems to lack a coherent intellectual framework for its reigning ideology. Where are the authoritative liberal intellectuals offering the philosophical principles and a thoughtful agenda for a better society? Is there a unifying theory to hold together its potent but unstable political coalition? Whereas a typical leftwing intellectual in the 20th century could describe his ideal society in some detail, even the most committed campus activist today appears hard pressed to answer basic questions about the long-term goals. Does *zhe/them* want the abolition of private property? What about the nuclear family? Are the ideologues comfortable with the *de facto* rule of Silicon Valley and Wall Street as long as those elites mouth the appropriate slogans, or will the final utopia dispense with its current oligarchic overclass? What would be the role of the United States in a triumphant woke world? Would it be an exporter and enforcer of modern, liberal values, or continue its economic and military decline and yield to various retrograde forces throughout the world? Are recalcitrant whites in the United States to be perpetually re-educated? What if that fails? Would they face expulsion from the regime? (Note the spontaneous cheering that seems to erupt at liberal gatherings when the latest census shows a continued decline in the white population.) That last option seems unlikely, however, not only because it sounds so extreme, but even more because it is hard to avoid the suspicion that the current ruling class *needs* its enemies. One consequence of the New Left and Mao Zedong's modification of Marxism in the 1960s and '70s was that permanent revolutionary struggle became an end in itself. Here may be another reason why most woke ideologues don't really know what kind of society they want: there *is* no final utopia – just the permanent revolution.

Meanwhile, the other half of America is united by a nostalgia for traditional morality and the founders' constitutionalism, but this seems too vague to serve as anything more than a temporary basis for self-defense against what they regard as an increasingly hostile regime.[4] Many self-described conservatives seem bewildered by the rapid transformation of American society. A perceptive observer noted in 2016 that the Left took Donald Trump literally but not seriously. We might say that the Right now takes leftwing ideology seriously but not literally: "How can they really believe those things?" Certainly it seems hard for traditionalists to accept that ordinary people – fellow Americans! – endorse, for example, letting five-year-olds decide whether to undergo surgical and chemical alteration of their gender identity.

The difficulty for the Right is that turning back the clock is not as easy as it sounds. If traditional, patriotic Americans could somehow win back political power, what would they do with it? In what ways would James Madison's republican government need to be adapted to the conditions of the 21st century? Which principles would remain the same and which would require updating in light of current geopolitics; social media; digital capitalism; medical, military, and transportation technology? Is there even agreement about something as essential as sexual morality? How many traditionalists would agree on the ideal state of family law? Would they go back to 1980? Or is that already too late? Perhaps 1930? 1780? Even many hard-core MAGA voters would find the moral restrictions of the founding era oppressive.

To the degree, therefore, that all sides may be in need of theoretical reflection about government, human nature, and man's place in the universe (including his relationship with God, if He exists), this book will consider some of the major developments in the western philosophical tradition that have shaped our current crisis. I also want to give a few brief examples at the end of the book that show how these theoretical issues have a direct bearing on our day-to-day lives. It would be going too far to say that G. W. Hegel is directly responsible for your clothes not getting clean in your energy-efficient washing machine, or for the paper straw that dissolves in your soda. (Still, there is a connection!) More ominously, these philosophical considerations can help us understand the excesses of the federal government's COVID restrictions, and the roots of our apparently permanent national surveillance state.

Chapter I

EXISTENTIAL WAR

There is a history in all men's lives
Figuring the nature of the times deceased,
The which observed, a man may prophesy,
With a near aim, of the main chance of things
As yet not come to life, which in their seeds
And weak beginnings lie intreasured.
Such things become the hatch and brood of time

Henry IV Part II, Act 3, scene 1

I DO NOT CLAIM any originality for the observations and suggestions that follow, which mainly try to draw together elements from different thinkers in a way that may be illuminating. Leo Strauss's essay "The Three Waves of Modernity" serves as a loose model, but with significant additions from other figures including Machiavelli, Fustel de Coulanges, Nietzsche, Michel Foucault, and Liu Xiaofeng, as well as several of my own teachers.[1] In each case I have tried to emphasize those observations that are most relevant for understanding our current dilemma.

A major reason our political crisis is so bitter and infuriating is that both sides increasingly regard each other as simply incomprehensible. The conservative writer Willmoore Kendall noticed decades ago that Left and Right were "venting upon each other the fury reserved for heretics," because each side is "in the eyes of the other, *heretical*."[2] The United States (in fact, the whole Western world) seems to be splitting into separate tribes, following different "gods," and thus different cosmologies. We no longer see reality in the same way, as Jonathan Haidt and many others have noted. Yet I'm not aware of any previous attempt to investigate this question in the way this short book attempts to do. My hope is that recognizing and accepting our divisions as ancient and theological – and thus resistant to rational discourse – could soften some of the frustration and confusion.

THE STATE OF THE LEFT

The United States seems to be ruled today as a post-constitutional regime, governed by a secular theology cobbled together from various modern European philosophers (predominantly, though not exclusively, Hegel, Marx, Nietzsche, and Heidegger). Yet the religion of the Woke Occupation preaches a strange catechism. If George Floyd is the faith's greatest martyr, its most authoritative prophet would seem to be Anthony Fauci. (It is possible that his stature will grow rather than diminish in retirement.) In November 2021, speaking on CBS's *Face the Nation*, Fauci said of his critics, "they're really criticizing science, because I represent science."[3] As the embodiment of science, of course, Fauci sanctified himself as a kind of public health oracle, whose authority exceeded any elected official in the federal government – including the occupant of the White House. Millions of the faithful obeyed Fauci's commandments with pious devotion. Unlike Moses, Fauci could claim no miracles to endow his authority with divine sanction. On the contrary, his pronouncements revealed all-too-human fallibility and inconsistency. Nevertheless, while racism constitutes the original sin of the woke religion, science represents its Holy Writ and promise of salvation. As noted above, these elements fit together uneasily, so much so that most interpretations of the Left's new religious impulse tend to focus on one aspect or the other, but rarely account for both.

And there are yet more difficulties. If the theology of the woke occupation has two distinct strands, it seems to comprise *three* political components: 1) a faction focused on racial grievances, represented by Critical Race Theory and Black Lives Matter, largely sustained and legitimized by the universities; 2) a militant anarcho-Marxist wing (most visibly manifest in Antifa) which receives rhetorical and organizational support from leftist members of Congress, radical mayors and district attorneys, and obscure financial backers; and 3) an elite, cosmopolitan oligarchy that exerts powerful influence on our public discourse, imposes its ideology on ever larger segments of the private sector, and swells the budgets of the militants with extravagant financial contributions. Clearly, the racial element of woke religiosity tracks with the Critical Race Theory component, while faith in science overlaps with the technocratic authority of the global oligarchy. Yet these factions represent very different interests and policy agendas. And there is still the anarcho-Marxist element to account for. How all these pieces fit together and who controls whom (or even *if* anyone is clearly in charge) are difficult questions, to say the least.

The chimera of woke religion and its Holy City of Antiracism likely won't be fully understood for some time. Yet there are some aspects that I think can be clarified through closer examination. Most of this book attempts to understand the

Left – both because it is the dominant political faction in America today, and because it most clearly represents modernity, with all its complexities and contradictions. My analysis of the Right will be largely confined to the next section. But before getting to that, one philosophical theme is worth exploring further. In his book *On the Genealogy of Morals*, Nietzsche refers to the "spirit of revenge" (or resentment) that grew out of Judaism and especially Christianity, with the Biblical emphasis on sin and the guilty conscience. In contrast to the Greeks and Romans, who glorified strength and political dominance, Christianity's defense of submission and weakness created a feeble and resentful priestly caste which ushered in a civilizational "transvaluation of values." The historical consequence of Christianity as the universal religion of the West was to displace the classic emphasis on splendor and nobility with a "slave morality." According to Nietzsche, Jesus's celebration of meekness led to the "interpretation of weakness itself... as *merit*."[4]

> The weakest are the ones who most undermine life among men, who most dangerously poison and question our trust in life.... They monopolize virtue now, these weak and incurably sick men, there is no doubt about that: "we alone are the good, the just." This is the way they speak.... As if health, good constitution, strength, pride, the sense of power were in themselves marks of depravity.... There is among them a plethora of vindictive men disguised as judges, whose mouths continually secrete the word "justice" like a poisonous saliva.... The will of the sick to display any form of superiority, its instinct for secret paths which lead to a tyranny over the healthy – where is it not to be found, this will to power of the weakest![5]

Many readers may see something familiar here. Nietzsche adds that these professional victims actually "enjoy being suspicious, grumbling over misdeeds and apparent insults, they rummage through the entrails of their past and present in search of dark, questionable stories which allow them to revel in a painful mistrust and to intoxicate themselves on their own malicious poison." Who does not recognize that? Consider in this context today's growing talk about reparations for slavery. Nietzsche said that these resentful souls "tear open the oldest wounds, they bleed from scars long healed, they make evildoers out of friends, wives, children, and whatever else is closest to them. 'I am suffering: someone must be to blame.'"[6] It is remarkable to consider that these words, which seem to describe today's grievance-mongers so well, were published in 1887.

Incidentally, Nietzsche explains that this attitude is entirely compatible with lusting for and wielding power. In fact, it can fit perfectly within a regime that aspires to be a global empire. Political greatness by itself does not make souls freer and more manly. "The man whose soul obeys the slavish command: 'Thou shalt and must kneel!'" may well crave participation in an unrestrained imperialism. He "will only bow all the more deeply and lick the dust more fervently."

Nietzsche's discussion is subtle and complex; he observes, for instance, that for all its grave flaws the new morality has produced depth and insight, and made human beings more interesting. But we cannot explore those intricacies here. The point is that Nietzsche accurately foresaw the contemporary phenomenon of imperious victimology: *et humiliter serviebant et superbe dominabantur* (humbly groveling while arrogantly ruling).

THE STATE OF THE RIGHT

The despotic rule of these woke "crybullies," everywhere evident today, is exasperating for many young white men who retain some sense of natural, spirited masculinity. More than that, there is a soul-destroying effect when those in charge ensure that these white "oppressors" are held back and excluded, all while being labeled as privileged supremacists. The resulting anger and cynicism have contributed to a powerful reaction against liberalism itself. To understand this sentiment it is helpful to note its similarity with the anti-liberal youth movement in Germany in the 1930s, which was examined with great insight by Leo Strauss in a famous 1941 lecture, "German Nihilism."

In this lecture Strauss analyzes the young militarists and nationalists in Germany who were disgusted by the spiritual bankruptcy of the Weimar Republic. They were often described as nihilists, but Strauss says that true nihilism is "the will to self-destruction," and he does not believe that "such a desire is the ultimate motive" of these young radicals. Their nihilism, such as it is, finds its expression, rather, in "a desire for the destruction of something specific: of modern civilization." While it is a mistake to explain this "in terms of a mental disease" or mere criminality, he also acknowledges that this "negation of modern civilization" is "not guided, or accompanied, by any clear positive conception." He describes this sense of negation as "a *moral* protest" based on the conviction that "a perfectly *open* society which is as it were the goal of modern civilization, and therefore all aspirations directed toward that goal, are irreconcilable with the basic demands of moral life." That means "all moral life is essentially and therefore eternally the closed society." The open society "is bound to be, if not immoral, at least amoral," and "is actually impossible." But in part because "they were unable to express in tolerably clear language what they desired to put in place of the present world" – that is, the specific conditions for a good life within a healthy political community – their passionate conviction "while not being nihilistic in itself... led however to nihilism."

What is the exact nature of the horror felt by these young people? Strauss described it as the prospect of a planetary society "devoted to production and consumption only" – "the production and consumption of spiritual as well as material merchandise." Because participation in such a society was so revolting to these young people, they could not imagine anything more contemptible than perpetuating the status quo. Seeing little future in "their own economic and social position" they believed "they had no longer anything to lose."

> What they hated was the very prospect of a world in which everyone would be happy and satisfied, in which everyone would have his little pleasure by day and his little pleasure by night, a world in which no great heart could beat and no great soul could breathe, a world without real, unmetaphoric, sacrifice, i.e. a world without blood, sweat, and tears.

To avoid that fate, "literally anything, the *nothing,* the chaos, the jungle, the Wild West, the Hobbian [*sic*] state of nature, seemed to them infinitely better." But however sincere or even understandable this feeling might be, Strauss insisted this movement suffered from a "fallacy" in its stubborn rejection of intelligent distinctions. These young people embraced a form of irrationalism, in part because all the authoritative emblems of "rational argument" seemed to consist of empty, pseudo-scientific "analysis" which was hardly more than "modern astrology."

Strauss, emphasizing again "that the nihilists were young people," exonerates them somewhat for being "unable to express in articulate language more than the negation of the aspirations of the older generation." A professor and advocate of liberal education might at this point be expected to blame these young people for not being properly brought up in the enlightened ideas of modern thought. Yet, on the contrary, Strauss emphasizes that their modern education was precisely the problem. "I am convinced that about the most dangerous thing for these young men was precisely what is called progressive education: they rather needed *old-fashioned teachers*, such old-fashioned teachers of course as would be undogmatic enough to understand the aspirations of their pupils." Those aspirations, recall, centered on an authentic moral life open to "great hearts and great souls," with "real, unmetaphoric sacrifice."

The only answer which could have impressed the young nihilists, had to be given in non-technical language. Only one answer was given which was adequate and which would have impressed the young nihilists if they had heard it. It was not however given by a German and it was given in the year 1940 only. Those young men who refused to believe that the period following the jump into liberty, following the communist world revolution, would be the finest hour of mankind in general and of Germany in particular, would have been impressed as much as we were, by what Winston Churchill said after the defeat in Flanders about Britain's finest hour.[7]

Churchill and the Allies vanquished the Nazis, and Strauss may well be right that the British statesman's rhetoric could have struck a chord with these lost young men. Yet Strauss would also remark in one of his books that the *philosophical* war of the mid-20th century had not been won as clearly as the *military* war. "It would not be the first time that a nation defeated on the battlefield and, as it were, annihilated as a political being, has deprived its conqueror of the most sublime fruit of victory, by imposing on him the yoke of its own thought."[8] The German Wehrmacht was obliterated, but the pernicious influence of certain German philosophers may in the long run prove to have been the greater threat.

For this reason, the American "tower of Babel" that Jonathan Haidt described needs to be understood in terms of the intense intellectual war that has been taking place in the background of day-to-day life. A helpful guide for understanding this is, perhaps surprisingly, a book written by a high-ranking member of the Chinese Communist Party. Wang Huning visited the United States in the late 1980s and in 1991 published *America Against America*, a detailed exploration of the many tensions that characterize American life. Since the publication of the book, Wang has risen to a prominent seat on the Chinese Politburo and is currently the highest-ranking theorist in the party. Despite being (presumably) an orthodox Marxist, Wang's book offers a sympathetic presentation of what traditional or conservative Americans believe. He understands, for instance, how the principles of the Declaration of Independence are understood by old-fashioned American citizens:

> The war of independence pushed equality to a new level, and subsequent developments have continued to advance

political equality. But equality in the economic and social spheres has been slow to advance because it is considered to be in the realm of liberty, and freedom is inviolable, especially the right to freedom of private property. Americans accept only equality of [opportunity], not equality of results. Once equality of [opportunity] is established, then comes the realm of liberty. Many Americans affirmed that [equality of opportunity] has been achieved and that any further talk of equality can only be about equality of results, which is an important reason why freedom has been the dominant value today.[9]

Unlike many of today's liberals, Wang is perfectly clear on the difference between the founders' political equality of natural rights and today's egalitarian, social-engineering equity (which is virtually the opposite of what Madison and Jefferson intended).

One of Wang's most important observations concerns the way Americans in the late 1980s preserved their civic heritage. After visiting Boston and Philadelphia, he astutely notes how the United States preserves its "historical displays of the founding." The United States, Wang notes, "excels" at making use of these "physical textbooks of political traditions." China, by contrast, has almost *too much* history compared to a young nation like the United States. Thus, "things that are not considered cultural relics by the Chinese are carefully protected" in the United States. "Americans not only preserve history" but use these sites for "spreading the American spirit." Wang understands and admires the importance of this "political education" for "long-lasting peace and stability." Of course, all that has changed dramatically in the last several decades. Wang himself notes near the end of the book, while discussing Allan Bloom's

The Closing of the American Mind (1987), that America was already in danger of losing its "spiritual" confidence and notes the possibility that American "society will fall into chaos and moral crisis."

One wonders if Wang might have been shocked by the destructive nihilism of the 2020 riots, and especially the radicals who destroyed America's historic monuments and statues during that same year. While the "spontaneous" demonstrations claimed to be a justified reaction to police racism, the toppling of statues and defacing of monuments represented a deliberate assault on America's political identity. No understanding of our current partisan divisions is possible without considering these acts of symbolic warfare on America's heritage. And as much as they revealed about the radical heart of the contemporary Left, equally important was the spineless reaction by most of the bipartisan political establishment. Traditional and conservative Americans understood in a profound, unmistakable way the message conveyed by the destruction itself, as well as the approval (implicit and often explicit) of the intellectual class and many politicians – including some Republicans.

Anticipating this phenomenon, Nietzsche observes that modern, liberal westerners treat their sophisticated awareness of the sins of the past as a personal burden. He compares this sense of historical guilt to a mass of indigestible stones in the belly. Whether or not one suffers from this particular affliction is a key difference between red and blue Americans. Thus, regardless of what one thinks of Donald Trump, he spoke for many old-fashioned citizens when he declared in a speech at Mount Rushmore on July 3, 2020, "No movement that seeks to dismantle these treasured American legacies can possibly have a love of America at its heart":

No person who remains quiet at the destruction of this resplendent heritage can possibly lead us to a better future.

The radical ideology attacking our country advances under the banner of social justice. But in truth, it would demolish both justice and society. It would transform justice into an instrument of division and vengeance, and it would turn our free and inclusive society into a place of repression, domination, and exclusion.

That probably represents as well as anything how traditional American citizens now see themselves and their country as under siege by the woke occupation.

With these considerations in mind, let us consider some broad themes in political philosophy that may prove useful.

Chapter II

THE CRISIS OF THE WEST AND THE SELF-DESTRUCTION OF REASON

HARRY NEUMANN, a profound but relatively obscure student of Leo Strauss, wrote in the late 1970s:

> The most important and most urgent question is how (or whether) to live. For its answer would determine the worth of raising any question.... Originally the solution to this problem was thought to be given by the gods, the ultimate moral authorities of one's family, tribe, or city. Since fear of these gods was the beginning of wisdom, any thought or act uninformed by this fear was experienced as impious and, therefore, bad. Socrates or some other Greek first contended that reason could liberate men from this fear by securing a detached, objective evaluation of his community's piety. Minds so liberated would be cosmopolitan and not tribal or civic in their moral orientation....
>
> Can philosophy or science do the job assigned to it by the Socratic tradition? Can it emancipate reason from the chains of old, inherited pieties? If not, why is it worthwhile to gratify the desire for freedom? Is that desire evil as Genesis (2:16–17) suggests?[1]

This question of the success or value of philosophy – and its repudiation by the Bible in Genesis – remains fundamental and unresolved, even today. Reflecting on this, we should recall that Socratic philosophy emerged out of what Neumann called "political rootedness." Political philosophy depends on and one might say "works with" settled moral habits and civic opinions. Yet there is always a precarious relationship between philosophy and politics, or "the philosopher and the city" (with the latter understood as the realm of morality and piety). Neumann argues that, without intending to, classical philosophy led to the destruction of politics, and thus dissolved the conditions for philosophical inquiry itself. The "utter annihilation of politics by science [was] philosophy's unintended culmination." This book is in part an attempt to work out what that suggestion means. For now, let me quote a passage from a different essay by Neumann, who, I should add, described himself as a nihilist convinced that the universe is utterly meaningless.

> I became aware of the crucial role of politics partly through arguments with Harry Jaffa and his best students. The status of politics is at the heart of their conflict with most of the other prominent students of Leo Strauss. Reflection on this fight has helped to clarify my own views. I came to see that Jaffa's enemies had much more in common with my nihilism or atheism than he did; Jaffa seems to me to be the real heir of Strauss's defense of politics against scientific or nihilistic devaluation. As a nihilist, I mean no disrespect when describing Jaffa's enemies as scientific and therefore nihilist. For this brings them closer than Jaffa or Strauss to what I regard as true. The only thing for which I fault them is unwillingness to recognize the atheism or nihilism inherent in their liberalism.[2]

Neumann and Jaffa represent what might be regarded as the farthest poles of possible interpretations of Leo Strauss's thought: Neumann revealed with a pitiless candor the inescapable consequences of modern nihilism; Jaffa displayed an unembarrassed patriotism and moral probity in defense of America. Both departed radically, though in different ways, from the conventional Straussians that Neuman cites. For this reason they might plausibly be considered Strauss's best, or worst, students. Perhaps neither of them represents the true understanding of Strauss's scholarship; yet to appreciate the full range of that scholarship I suggest we must take seriously the implications of what Neumann and Jaffa contend. By chance or providence, both of these heterodox Strauss students were colleagues and taught for many years in the Claremont consortium of colleges in southern California.[3] For decades, they led a popular joint seminar, "Socrates or Nihilism," in which Jaffa defended classical rationalism and Neumann exposed our modern Nietzschean world without fig leaves.

Both Neumann and Jaffa held that Strauss's overt concern was to recover the possibility of political philosophy, which they both regarded as an emphatically political and even moral project. This need to recover political philosophy was driven by what Strauss many times referred to as "the crisis of the West."

In his "Three Waves of Modernity" essay, Strauss explains that for the ancient and medieval thinkers, "Nature supplies the standard, a standard wholly independent of man's will.... Man has his place in an order which he did not originate." But in the first wave of what is often called "the modern project," Machiavelli, Descartes, and Thomas Hobbes rejected this view in the name of science. The classical philosophers, particularly Plato and Aristotle, were anti-utopian because they recognized the limits of reason in civic life. Passion, self-interest, and superstition will always stand in the way of perfect justice. But as Strauss explains, for the modern thinkers writing during the early phase of the Renaissance and scientific revolution, "the political problem becomes a technical problem" because "man's power is infinitely greater than was hitherto believed[;] man's perfection is not the natural end of man but an ideal freely formed by man." This was followed by the second wave, originating with Rousseau and culminating in Hegel, which turns from science to History as the solution to human imperfection. Rationality came to be understood as embodied in the historical process, and the "end of History" (culminating in the Prussian state of the 19th century, according to Hegel) revealed the final answers to political life. But the stubborn persistence of war, ignorance, and misery deflated the belief in progress – which led to Nietzsche and the third wave. This next step was characterized by "the experience of terror and anguish" that erupts when History fails to deliver the promised utopia, and we are forced to abandon "the now baseless belief in the rationality or progressive character of the historical process."

This rush through several centuries of philosophical thought might seem hard to follow for non-specialists, and we will discuss it in more detail below. The key point for now is that today's intellectual class can offer no rational alternative to postmodern relativism and nihilism. "The crisis of modernity," Strauss explains,

> reveals itself in the fact, or consists in the fact, that modern western man no longer knows what he wants – that he no longer believes that he can know what is good and bad, what is right and wrong. Until a few generations ago, it was generally taken for granted that man can know what is right and wrong, what is the just or the good or the best

order of society – in a word that political philosophy is possible and necessary. In our time this faith has lost its power.

This might seem like an odd statement, or even obviously wrong in light of the extreme, not to say fanatical, moral certainty of America's ruling orthodoxy. Aren't we bombarded every day with official declarations of right and wrong? But Strauss was not claiming that no one believes in anything. What he meant is that we no longer believe any account of justice or morality can be rational, trans-cultural, trans-historical, and – it seems necessary to add today – trans-racial. Modern educated westerners no longer accept that there can be a theoretically true account of what is good for man, and in particular an account of political justice for human beings as such, understood not necessarily as a practical goal, but as a universal standard across time and distance.

That is why Strauss goes on to say the crisis of modernity is "primarily the crisis of modern political philosophy." Strauss was aware that this could seem like a self-serving statement by a scholar who views all problems through the lens of his own research: "why should the crisis of a culture primarily be the crisis of one academic pursuit among many?" But, Strauss explains,

> political philosophy is not essentially an academic pursuit: the majority of the great political philosophers were not university professors. Above all, as is generally admitted, modern culture is emphatically rationalistic, believing in the power of reason; surely if such a culture loses its faith in reason's ability to validate its highest claims, it is in crisis.[4]

This again may seem to be an odd or inaccurate statement, for leftist ideology (e.g. "feminist glaciology"[5]) is certainly

characterized in large part by its *rejection* of objective rationality. Since the 1980s' campus slogan, "Hey, hey, ho-ho, Western
Culture's got to go," up through today's derision of mathematics
as an essentially arbitrary imposition of white hegemony, the
radical Left has been turning its back on Eurocentric notions of
rational thought, particularly that form of rationalism that orig-
inated in ancient Athens and culminated, to some degree, in the
Enlightenment. Oddly enough, as Strauss will explain, this
rejection of reason, this anti-rationalism – which in its most
extreme form becomes nihilism – arises out of Socratic philosophy itself.

While the dead-end of modern philosophy was evident to
thinkers such as Nietzsche and Heidegger a century ago, on the
popular level the political and social crisis of modernity seemed
to reach a climax in the 1960s. Even more pernicious than the
hippie counter-culture was the New Left, which rejected tolerance and progress as sentimental distractions, and embraced
revolution as an end in itself. Ronald Reagan's muscular patriotism and forceful prosecution of the Cold War put leftism on
its heels, but this might have been only temporarily if not for
the somewhat unexpected disintegration of the Soviet Union
between 1989 and 1991, which knocked all the trends off-track.
Then, as Americans were enjoying their economic and psychic
"peace dividend," another surprise – the attacks of 9/11 – restored
some genuine feelings of national unity while antiquating the
fifty-year-old fixed fortifications of Left versus Right in foreign
policy, and even on some domestic issues. Only after the raid that
killed Osama bin Laden in May 2011, and Barack Obama's official announcement of the end of the global war on terror in May
2013, did the domestic quarrel over the culture begin to return
from its quarter-century interregnum. Trump's arrival on the

scene coincided with, or perhaps signaled in some way, the battle over America's soul picking up where it left off in the late 1980s. Today's Critical Race Theory is just Reagan-era deconstructionism and Afrocentrism emerging from hibernation.

If this speculation – about a twenty-five-year hiatus in the cultural cold war – is valid, it would help explain an odd generational disconnect on the Right. Many anti-woke young people are disgusted by what they see as the complacency of conservative "boomers." But those who lived through the 1980s may seem more equanimous because they regard today's leftist intolerance as merely a second act of the political correctness of the 1980s and early '90s. The main difference for this older generation might be that today's version is *less* impressive, since it is accompanied by so much of the self-pity mentioned above. Who – the older generation wonders – can take seriously these safe-space soldiers and sunshine snowflakes? To be sure, the rot seems to have spread into corporate America and even, to some degree, into the military, but these institutions have always managed to bow to fashions while still carrying on with their essential functions. The boomers think, "We've *been* through all this already. Political correctness didn't stop us from beating the Russkies and winning the war on terrorism. Along the way, we've seen Republican and Democratic presidents come and go; yet the United States is still here."

This is not the place to adjudicate that dispute; and events are too fluid in any case to draw any definite conclusions about where the nation is headed. But if my hypothesis is correct about the militant New Left simply going underground for a few decades, then many of the most penetrating analyses from the 1970s and '80s could still be relevant. Given how many Americans remain bewildered by what's happening right now, these older writings could allow us to step back and see our present difficulties from a broader perspective.

Two schools of thought from that era seem especially relevant. First, Leo Strauss and his students offered a powerful diagnosis of the crisis in modern politics, which they see as arising fundamentally from a crisis in modern philosophy. Second, to the degree that we are living in a world radically shaped by continental philosophy, we need to understand it from the inside, so to speak. In a post-Nietzschean universe, how do we understand the social sciences, which make it "possible both to protect life and to authorize a holocaust"?[6] The writings of Michel Foucault, who died in 1984, represent and help to explain this intellectual climate.

WHY STRAUSS?

It is necessary to say a few words in defense of what has so far only been presumed, namely that Leo Strauss was indeed the most formidable critic of modern philosophy in our time and one of the best guides for navigating the crisis we face. Jaffa believed that Strauss had attempted nothing less than a complete refutation of the modern (or Machiavellian) project. "As far as I know, Strauss was the first, or at least the most radical, of those who have challenged this entire enterprise – in perhaps 400 years." All previous critics, including Rousseau, Nietzsche, and Heidegger, according to Jaffa, "have done so, either originally or in the end, on the basis of a more radical modernity. Strauss alone, so far as I know, has challenged modernity... from a point of view absolutely detached from its roots and its branches."[7]

This view finds support from an unexpected quarter. As mentioned above, Wang Huning's 1991 *America Against America* discusses in some detail *The Closing of the American Mind* by Allan Bloom, another Strauss student. Nowadays, Wang keeps a lower profile as a leading intellectual in the Chinese Communist Party. But there is burgeoning interest in Strauss's writings throughout the Chinese academic world, led primarily by Professors Gan Yang and Liu Xiaofeng. In an essay published in English in 2016, Professor Liu raises the question of why Chinese scholars are interested in Strauss.

> Faced with this question, I have my own perplexities. In Western universities, Strauss's thought is not a very trendy topic, but the Chinese intellectual community has indeed paid much attention to him. Some scholars have a skeptical or even hostile attitude towards him. This is indeed natural. What baffles me is that, when we introduce more prominent theories by people such as Michel Foucault, John Rawls, Jürgen Habermas, Friedrich Hayek, and Jacques Derrida, I do not hear Western scholars ask why we introduce them; nor have Chinese scholars expressed such a doubtful or fiercely opposing attitude. Why does the relatively less prominent Strauss alone cause such a fuss?

Liu suggests that there is something qualitatively and self-consciously different about Strauss's approach to political philosophy:

> How is it possible that modern thinkers are all wrong save Strauss? This is a good question, and is of the same nature as the one I posed earlier: what is wrong with studying

modern theories? These questions are certainly directed toward Strauss himself. And the answer should be found by carefully studying his writings. Strauss was aware of these questions, and had already carefully explicated his answer....

By reintroducing the perspective of classical political philosophy, Strauss reminds us that the attitude towards democracy and a universal enlightenment was already an extremely important subject of debate in classical Greek political philosophy. Reviewing ancient thought enables us to cautiously reconsider various political problems....

In the present, Western philosophy in Chinese academia is dominated by phenomenology, analytic philosophy, hermeneutics, and deconstructionism, all of which have their foundations in Enlightenment thought. In contrast, Strauss's political philosophy is based on the Platonic tradition, and weaves into itself the entire history of Western thought. His scholarly works are mostly interpretations of writings of the past, or introductory pieces that important professors do not care to write.

Liu sums up the core issue by noting that Strauss's "strategy is to go back to classical works of political philosophy. He revives the problematization of the trial of Socrates."[8]

I believe Liu is correct, and that Strauss considered the "problem of Socrates" to be somehow fundamental to human life. If the modern project was an attempt to reject or overcome that problem, and if that project has failed, we seem to have no choice but to turn our attention back to the beginning.

PLATO AND THE DANGER OF
PHILOSOPHIC TYRANNY

*Eros lives like a tyrant within him in all anarchy and law-
lessness; and, being a monarch, will lead the man whom it
controls, as though he were a city, to every kind of daring.*

PLATO, *Republic* 575a

Among political philosophers, the issue of whether Socrates was
guilty – whether Athens was justified in executing him – is an old
and controversial question. For most modern westerners (including many Straussians), the answer is settled: the principles of
tolerance, intellectual freedom, and philosophical skepticism
are almost sacrosanct. What, after all, is the opposite of "closing
the American mind"? Yet Thomas West and Harry Neumann, to
name two prominent scholars of political philosophy, have
argued that Socrates's conviction was legitimate, and Athens
acted reasonably. Strauss wrote, "Socrates, in particular, was a
very conservative man as far as the ultimate practical conclusions of his political philosophy were concerned." Yet the Greek
playwright "Aristophanes pointed to the truth by suggesting
that Socrates's fundamental premise could induce a son to beat
up his own father, i.e., to repudiate in practice the most natural
authority."[9] Harry Neumann asserts that Socrates's accusers
"perceived the atheistic implications" of his philosophizing. Thus,
"the question of the rightness of the condemnation of Socratic
atheism by pious Athenians, remains *the* question of Western
civilization."[10] I suspect that Strauss not only acknowledged
the legitimacy of Athens's judgment against Socrates, but that
on a certain level he even regarded *Plato* as guilty.

But what would Plato be guilty of, exactly?

As Socrates's greatest defender, the author of the *Republic* – the world's most famous work of philosophy – elevated the role of reason in human life more forcefully and more successfully than any figure in history. Plato, we might say, was the ultimate champion of freedom of thought, unfettered by any sacred or traditional taboos. Platonic philosophy, to use a famous formulation from his dialogues, seeks to replace opinion with knowledge about the greatest questions: virtue and happiness, wisdom and friendship, being and nature, the soul and the cosmos. Plato's specific, though not exclusive, focus on human concerns meant, in part, that he was primarily not a natural scientist or metaphysician but a political philosopher.

On the one hand, it seems that nothing could be more beneficial than Plato's rationalism. As Harry Jaffa liked to point out, we all want to be guided by the most intelligent and knowledgeable doctors and lawyers. The same principle would seem to hold with political leaders: we want the wisest to be in charge. Isn't every aspect of life, in fact, improved when we make decisions based on logic and facts rather than unthinking assumptions? Insofar as Plato paved the way to discredit brutal customs, irrational hatreds, and mindless superstitions, humanity owes him a great debt. On the other hand, Plato's project led to some... difficulties. Already, a faint line pointing toward the paradoxes of modern Leftism is beginning to emerge. But first, it is necessary to give Plato his due, even if all too inadequately.

Political philosophy is not inevitable in any deterministic way, according to Strauss, and could even be suppressed by a global tyranny. Yet it does seem to arise naturally:

It is true that political life is concerned primarily with the individual community to which the people happen to belong, and mostly even with individual situations, whereas political philosophy is concerned primarily with what is essential to all political communities. Yet there is a straight and almost continuous way leading from the pre-philosophic to the philosophic approach. Political life requires various kinds of skills, and in particular that apparently highest skill which enables a man to manage well the affairs of his political community as a whole.[11]

Once a community achieves a certain level of political and economic maturity – including the leisure for reflection – it will begin to study and cultivate the "the art, the prudence, the practical wisdom [of] the excellent statesman or politician." In other words, political science will likely emerge. For the moment, we can treat political science and political philosophy as equivalent. Both seek, at least in part, those principles that promote sound political decisions in a wide variety of situations – the kind of knowledge that Strauss calls "transferable" because it applies to all political life. Because political philosophy teaches what is transferable, that knowledge is universal, which necessarily implies a common standard by which to judge sound or healthy politics. In classical political philosophy this universal standard of political morality or justice is *natural right*. That is, the various opinions about justice derived from local customs can be evaluated by a rational inquiry into what is right by nature. Since all politics involves human beings, who share a common nature, knowledge of human nature and natural right is what makes political science transferable or universal.

This all seems straightforward. Yet, to return to the problem, Plato's teacher was executed by the citizens of Athens precisely because of his relentless and profane questions about the rational grounds of justice and truth. Of course, modern man is too enlightened for that. We no longer penalize anyone for

25

challenging the regime's opinions about justice. We don't imprison people for crimes against orthodoxy or "sacred" doctrines, symbols, and customs – or so modern liberals like to believe. A modern democracy is not supposed to create religious martyrs and saints, criminalize impiety, or declare those who worship false gods to be "domestic terrorists."

What seemed at first perhaps a bit absurd – that the fate of one argumentative Greek philosopher 2,500 years ago could have any bearing on America's current political crisis – may now seem slightly more plausible. Plato is, in crucial respects, the original instigator of our cold civil war; and elements of both Left and Right are enacting and rebelling against Plato's legacy.

Both Right and Left are *enacting* Plato's legacy because they are still operating, in important ways, within modern rationalism at its broadest and most optimistic. For the mainstream Right, this includes the major features of republicanism: consent, constitutional limited government, religious liberty, and national sovereignty, as well important elements of traditional morality including the integrity of the family.

Of course, as discussed above, some significant elements of the Right are breaking away from some of these features of classical liberalism. Among many younger people on the Right, there is considerable interest today in various anti-modern thinkers who disdain the hollowness of bourgeois commercialism: Julius Evola, Ernst Jünger, Yukio Mishima, and especially Carl Schmitt – who is probably the most original and influential of such writers, and famously defined the core of politics as the distinction between friends and enemies. Civic piety, from this perspective, is characterized most fundamentally by whom one loves and hates.[12] Harry Neumann cogently describes this attitude, which is not confined to the Right:

When, for example, feminists and sexists, democrats and nazis, hate each other, they see their enemies as evil, truly evil. Their hatred, if justified as they are convinced it is, implies a god, an eternal, nonarbitrary standard of good and evil. Men with shared gods (moral absolutes) unite against enemies. Politics always has been, and always will be, this belligerent determination to empower one's gods, to ram them down the enemy's throat by legal enactment enforced by police-military power. Politics is legislated morality (religion). Carl Schmitt, citing Donoso Cortez, rightly insisted: Without theology, no morality and without morality, no politics! [13]

The Left, at least at the level of slogans, still professes allegiance to many liberal principles such as equality (or equity), cosmopolitanism, universal human rights, etc. This is certainly true of the oligarchic and even to some degree the Marxist elements within the woke coalition. There are some difficulties, however, with the third element, which is obsessed with ethnocentric antiracism. Crusades of moral righteousness seem to fill a deep psychological need, by supplying the communal bonds, moral seriousness, and spiritual zeal found in the closed and intimate societies of the ancient world. To understand this yearning for a holy city, it might help to see this reaction against Plato's cosmopolitan legacy as in one sense a mirror of Plato's own "Weimar problem." If space permitted, there would be a fascinating story to tell here about the political situation in 5th-century B.C. Athens, which involved the devastating effects of the Peloponnesian War, the corrosive influence of materialistic philosophy *prior* to Socrates, and Athens's own "loss of faith." [14] Instead, a thumbnail sketch will have to suffice. Jaffa described the matter this way:

27

The gods of the ancient city were no longer a believable ground for morality, for Socrates no less than for the pre-Socratics. They remained believable, however, for ordinary citizens, for whom the identification of morality with belief in their ancestral gods also remained, and would so remain very largely until the advent of Christianity. For Socrates and for his followers, however, the ideas – the intelligible necessities underlying the being or goodness of things – replaced the gods as the ultimate authority.[15]

That is to say, for the intellectual elite – the aristocratic, open-minded young men that Plato hoped to cultivate as students – the anthropomorphic (and somewhat unbelievable) Olympian gods would give way to the Forms or Ideas: the intelligible "beings" by which we can make sense of the cosmos. The problem was (according to Neumann and others) that Plato's intention, or "conspiracy," slipped its leash. His bold free-thinking and dabbling with utopian theories did not remain confined to his caste of educated gentlemen. In fact, the plan for keeping philosophy "aristocratic" turned out be a rather dismal failure – or at least Machiavelli, and Nietzsche, thought so.

The attempt to popularize philosophic education, the ambitious conceit at the heart of the Enlightenment, might seem altruistic. But this project becomes extremely dangerous if there is – as Plato suggests – a kind of tyrannical impulse lurking in the philosopher's uninhibited *eros*. The unbridled pursuit of theoretical wisdom, the desire to answer the "what is" questions with the greatest possible precision, points toward constructing – *at first* only in speech – a perfect city. The city, or regime, is the most interesting and accessible "whole" within the greater whole of the universe: literally a *microcosm*. (One of Strauss's students,

Seth Benardete, called political philosophy the "eccentric core" of philosophy.) Moreover, a theoretically perfect utopia is not made less ideal, from the philosophic point of view, by the fact that no one would want to live there.

Stanley Rosen, another unorthodox Straussian, has written that the *Republic* "is a kind of surrogate fulfillment of Plato's political ambitions." The dialogue "is itself a revolutionary political act that sets into motion the historical dialectic of politics and philosophy. Plato expresses simultaneously the need of politics for philosophy and the danger of each for the other." The *Republic*, Rosen adds, is "perhaps the most influential cause" of what would ultimately lead to the horrors of the 20th century: "the deterioration of philosophy into ideology." Plato's bracing and enchanting dialogues depicting the grandeur of philosophy reflect, perhaps even encourage, a terrible enticement: philosophers, or those who regard themselves as philosophers, would "compel themselves" to *rule*, which "usually if not always leads to disastrous results."[16] (This may be one reason Strauss turned his attention to the "bashful" Xenophon in his final books on Xenophon's Socratic writings – where he notes that Xenophon portrays Socrates as rather pedestrian, emphasizing his practicality over his theoretical wisdom.[17] In his 1963 Xenophon course, Strauss even calls Plato's rhetoric "crude" and "obvious," and thus suggests Plato is responsible for philosophy becoming *too* successful, a point he makes explicitly in his "Restatement" on the *Hiero*.[18])

Rosen and other Straussians use the term *rule* in a broad sense. In the *Republic*'s well-known metaphor of the cave, the true "legislators" are those who create the flickering images on the cave wall – those who shape the regime's authoritative opinions about the sacred, the noble, and the just, taught through epic stories and myths. The philosophic legislator, or tyrant (insofar as he is above the law), rules indirectly but nevertheless powerfully, not with a sword, one might say, but with a shadow. In the *Republic*, the old poets (storytellers) are expelled, but only to be replaced by others under the close supervision of the philosophers. "When the poets depict the gods they must no longer look to laughter and pity but to the ideas," writes Allan Bloom in his commentary on the dialogue.[19]

Clearly, many of the most urgent themes in our contemporary politics are already brought out in Plato – including the power of ideas (for good or ill), the balance between wisdom and consent, and the question of who writes the ruling stories or "narratives" that determine political reality. During a class on Plato's *Apology* and *Crito* in 1966, Strauss raised this issue of Plato's relevance, particularly with regard to the role of expertise in a democracy:

> Can one clarify this issue – democracy or rule of experts – without understanding experts in the light of philosophers? For the following reason: experts are, as everybody knows, specialists, which means partial knowers. Now the partial, the incomplete, cannot be properly understood except in the light of the complete. And the complete knower, at least according to their claim, to his claim, is the philosopher. So I think we will not completely disregard our immediate political problems by considering such a seemingly far-fetched issue.[20]

The "complete knower" – that, in a way, is the problem in a nutshell.

It should be evident by now that in raising these themes it

30

has not been my purpose to condemn philosophy or Plato – particularly since I have no standing to attempt anything so preposterous. I do, however, want to share some of the critiques of Plato's rhetorical or dialectical openness. Among academic Straussians it is a commonplace to refer to the "tension between the philosopher and city." As Strauss himself warned, however, such formulations have a tendency to lapse into cliches and thereby lose their revelatory power. Students of political philosophy risk complacency and dogmatism when they forget the danger implied in that tension. Natural right is "dynamite," as Strauss reminded us. What this means, however, is a matter of some dispute.

REFLECTION AND CHOICE OR THE HOLLOW STATE

Several prominent Straussians have suggested, or more than suggested, that the "terrible truth" uncovered by philosophers – *all* philosophers – is nihilism.[21] According to this view, there is always a latent conflict between philosophic skepticism and the city's need for fixed moral rules and authoritative traditions, because philosophy always reveals those rules and traditions to be completely groundless. The irony or comedy of the *Republic*, in this view, consists in the philosophic discovery that every actual regime rests entirely on myth and absurdity. Jaffa would respond (together with the authors of the *Federalist Papers*) that of course all political communities are imperfect, inasmuch as they are always mixtures of natural and conventional justice, which is why civic loyalty needs the support of patriotic stories and traditions.

The nihilist position, however, argues that *all* justice is *entirely* conventional, without any natural or divine support. To the degree that anything is right according to nature, it is only the philosopher's unflinching confrontation with the stark reality of cosmic nothingness. If I seem to be exaggerating, consider Thomas Pangle's introduction to Leo Strauss's *Studies in Platonic Political Philosophy*: "All men other than the philosopher, one may say, live lives that are tragic or comic or both"; they are "in the most important respects deluded boasters, skaters on thin ice unable or unwilling to look down for very long" at what lies beneath their feet. The philosopher, by contrast, is distinguished by being able to liberate himself "from every delusion or false hope" and "bask in the austere light" of the truth.

This contention that all philosophers are nihilists seems implausible for both textual and common-sensical reasons. Consider Aristotle's arguments connecting virtue with happiness, a view widely supported by most reasonable people. As Jaffa put it: "Aristotle says at the beginning of the Seventh Book of the *Politics* that the man who was a perfect coward, who was frightened by anything, and who would sacrifice his best friend, who was so intemperate that in order to get food or sex he would sacrifice anyone or anything for his immediate appetite, would be a miserable human being. I think we do have rational knowledge of the highest degree of certitude as to the value of the basic moral virtues for a good life."[22] Moreover, insofar as a nihilistic rejection of morality becomes merely dogmatic, it abandons Socrates's *zetetic* or skeptical philosophizing, which always remains open to the fundamental alternatives.

The textual evidence is supplied in part by Pangle's own imagery, which echoes Nietzsche: nothingness is darkness, the abyss, the murky depths beneath the thin ice. Plato famously describes political life – which is always partially hidden from the truth by myths – as a cave. Yet, equally famously, he describes philosophic wisdom not as a *descent* into a subterranean void but as an *ascent*. The truth is above, on the surface where living things grow and are illuminated in the light of the sun, revealing the truth of the beings – a truth that is blinding not by its darkness but by its brightness. Undiluted natural right, according to Jaffa (and, I believe, Strauss), is explosive not because it masks cosmic emptiness, but because perfect justice is too potent, too demanding, for man's imperfect nature. Philosophers must guard the "terrible truth" because the pure justice discerned by reason, when liberated from prudence, removes not the sail but the anchor of stable political life.

These arguments are not intended to, and can't really, *prove* whether or not philosophic wisdom ends in nihilism. It is in the nature of philosophy itself that such matters can never be definitively settled through ordinary language. Harry Jaffa, while certainly disagreeing with such a conclusion, acknowledged that Strauss's "refutation of historicism can lead to a blind nihilism, and for many, including many Straussians, it has done so."[23] In the end, it may be that each of us must make a moral choice.

THE PROBLEM OF POLITICAL KNOWLEDGE

The average suits everybody and fits nobody.

Seth Benardete[24]

To come back to the main argument, perhaps this Promethean fire of the Idea of Justice, discovered by philosophical insight, *can* be controlled – in the right hands and under the right circumstances, of course. The philosopher's tyrannical temptation, as Stanley Rosen argues, supposes that his superior knowledge of nature, justice, and the human soul – not to mention a mastery of rhetoric and refutation – can supply the complete political art. Having gained this hard-won understanding through intense contemplation and dialectical reasoning, why *not* put the direct rule of wisdom into practice?[25] Becoming a tyrant would provide the philosopher with fascinating experimental data.[26] As for the famous claim that philosophers do not wish to rule, that may, after all, be only an assertion by the philosophers themselves to mask their ambition.

Plato explores several of these themes in a lesser-known dialogue titled the *Statesman*. It is the third in a series, preceded by the *Theaetetus* and the *Sophist*. For most of the dialogue, there are only two principal characters: a mathematician called Young Socrates (adult Socrates speaks briefly then withdraws) and an older philosopher known as the Eleatic Stranger. Plato's purpose, as Mark Blitz explains, is to "define the *politikos*, whom we may call the statesman, the political man, the political scientist, or the political knower." The dialogue explores "the place of knowledge in political life – in human life – and the ways to combine things, politically and more generally."[27]

Whereas the *Republic* is sweeping and majestic, full of arresting images, Strauss describes the *Statesman* as "ugly."[28] It drags us through false starts, dead-ends, errors, and digressions. Plato makes the dialogue frustrating or even unpleasant to read, and its characters lurch through a long, circuitous route before they even clarify the subject matter of statesmanship and especially the statesman's particular form of knowledge. The difficulties that run through this bucket-of-bolts dialogue might be seen as a counterpoint to the beauty of the impossible

Republic. There is, we find, no arithmetical precision in the art of politics, only a large measure of messiness, perhaps even futility.[29]

So far from reenforcing the claim advanced in the *Republic* that wisdom is the only legitimate claim to rule, the *Statesman* can be seen as repudiating a science of statesmanship altogether. According to Seth Benardete, it even "vindicates political philosophy by holding political science up to ridicule."[30] This critique of political knowledge – which apparently cannot be simultaneously exact and complete – comes out in at least two major features of the dialogue.

First, Young Socrates is shown the insufficiency of his mathematical expertise with a demonstration that human beings and their political needs are hard to measure properly: the best statesman weaves together disparate human virtues (moderation and courage) and contrapuntal political necessities (the justice of equality and the justice of excellence) – qualities that are not only incommensurate, but which cannot even be reckoned in the same way.[31] The city needs both sameness and difference, homogeneity and heterogeneity, yet these do not always intersect neatly. Second, the dialogue's interlocutors seem oddly unable to divide evenly, and thus cannot properly define what sort of creatures the statesman governs. They work through a convoluted and somewhat ridiculous taxonomy to settle finally on man as a specific type of herd animal – both pig-like and bird-like. The inadequate jocularity of this definition is confirmed by two cosmological myths the Stranger relates, which contrast the statesman's art with the direct, benevolent rule of a god over sub-humans.

Taken as a whole, the dramatic action of the dialogue seems to indicate by counter-argument that the carnivorous interest the shepherd has in his flock is not a suitable analogue to lawgiving among men. In a typically Platonic way, the dialogue *shows* (rather than merely asserting through the speeches) that proper statesmanship resists any comprehensive and precise methodology. Again, the experience of reading the dialogue is crucial, because Plato instructs us not only through the words of the characters, but through what Jacob Klein calls "the uneasy feeling that is the result of the disorderliness, impreciseness, and faultiness" of the dramatic presentation.[32]

Michel Foucault (who read Greek and maintained a long-standing interest in classical philosophy) sees Plato's statesman as neither all-knowing scientist nor all-caring shepherd, both of which exceed a reasonable expectation of political knowledge. Yet, Foucault – like Nietzsche, Neumann, and Rosen – thought Plato's rationalism played a part in the modern attempt to exercise totalitarian "pastoral" power over human beings.[33]

Of course, the *Statesman*, like all Platonic dialogue, "deals with the whole by implication,"[34] and there seems to be a deeper level related to the knowledge of being, or ontology. By weighing the arguments in their dramatic context, one could say that Plato is making the case against scientific government as part of, or on the way to, an argument against a scientific ontology. Young Socrates and the Stranger show that the attempt to reduce the political art to a single method or rational system cannot succeed, thereby revealing a lesson for the legislator of the Ideas, or the aspiring metaphysician.

No systematic code can nail down either justice or being. Partly this is because of the limitations of speech: "Further, on account of the weakness of language," Plato says in his Seventh Letter, it is impossible "to show what each thing is like, not less than what each thing is. For this reason no man of intelligence will venture to express his philosophical views in language, especially not in language that is unchangeable, which is true of that which is set down in written characters." (In this sense, the doctrine of the Forms or Ideas is itself a partial or distorted account, a shadow play.)

In a 1966 course on Plato's *Meno*, Strauss explains how Plato deals with this problem:

> Plato likes the term "divining." We all divine much more than we clearly see.... Now such divining underlies all laws, all authoritative opinions. These laws and authoritative opinions – that is the core of what now is called a culture or a civilization – differ "historically," meaning from epoch to epoch and from nation to nation. Yet they all have in common – despite their immense variety and the immense differences of rank – they all have in common the same kind of origin.

Strauss here mentions the role of founders, and then continues: "Now they all have the same kind of origin in another sense of the term origin, namely, in the truth. As Plato would put it, they all divined the ideas to different degrees." Because they "all divined fragments of the truth," Strauss says that "to this extent, they are all genuine. They become merely convention only by the act of absolutization," when they harden into sacred laws and customs (*nomoi*) that cannot be questioned.

Politically, the absolutization of truth is necessary – insofar as the ordinary, non-theoretical citizens understand truth. This solid ground seems necessary for the philosopher also, who begins with examining the city's fundamental law, though he will necessarily challenge and seek to go beyond this pious orthodoxy (which Strauss calls "divination which has been frozen"). Yet absolute certainty seems deadly as well as necessary, not only to philosophy but also to the city.

On the one hand, skepticism is the heart of Socratic philosophy, which must always resist dogmatic certainty. Yet the philosopher would become paralyzed if he doubted absolutely the reliability of his own senses or the intelligibility of the world. The pursuit of wisdom presupposes that some knowledge is possible. Likewise, statesmen cannot wait on the musings of speculative thinkers. Political men must act on the basis of reasonably certain knowledge, while citizenship generally requires uncomplicated respect for the sanctity of the law. Nevertheless, men of practical affairs must remain flexible about even the fundamental law. A slavish obedience to tradition can lead in some circumstance to the regime's self-destruction. Necessity requires that prudence consider all possible options.[35]

The citizens must be united by an unshakeable common faith in the nature of the world and the basic justice of their regime, or there will not be sufficient unity to hold the city together. At the same time, the disjointed goods that define the human condition – the fact that politics always labors to combine imperfectly different demands – means political knowledge and political rule must practice moderation in both aspiration and deed.

Harry Jaffa formulated this idea, as it appears in the self-understanding of American citizenship, in this way: "A free society is undoubtedly 'pluralistic.' But pluralism implies diversity within unity. It cannot be an unbounded diversity." *E pluribus unum*, the motto of the United States, refers to the many states joining in Union. But it also "refers, less obviously but more profoundly, to the moral unity that underlies the moral diversity comprehended by the same Union."[36]

Thus, the art of lawgiving – as we also learn in Plato's *Minos* – does not consist only in writing a sound constitution; there must also be some metaphysical and cosmological background that provides an orderly framework for the world. The city needs a civil religion, or what Socrates in Book IV of the *Laws* calls "preludes" to the laws. (Benardete's commentary on the dialogue calls them "definitional laws."[37]) These explanatory justifications "tune" the souls of the citizens to accept the authority of the *nomoi* willingly.[38] Law therefore seems to be inseparable from ontology both up and down.[39] Every righteous city requires a firm (if partly conventional) metaphysical foundation beneath it. Likewise, the philosopher ascending from the authoritative opinions must "pass through the city" (as Benardete says) in his ascent to the "what is" questions, or the understanding of being.[40]

Let me add one additional point which brings us back to the theme of knowledge and tyranny. In the *Statesman* the Stranger argues that any prolonged absence of the legislator from the city leads to a breakdown in the law; he may therefore find it necessary to alter the laws on his return. Here Plato seems to suggest a reciprocal relationship between what is and the *account* of what is – or between being and *logos*.[41] When we add the *Statesman's* teaching that the art of the statesman is to command – to be the technical creator or artificer of the laws – we seem to come close to something like Heideggerian existentialism: the human account of reality *is* reality, in crude terms.

And yet precisely Plato's insistence on cutting political knowledge down to size indicates another way of understanding this relationship between man and being, which is shown in the dubiousness of the shepherd model. The statesman does not rule completely because man is not merely a herd animal. Likewise, any theoretical account, or *logos*, of being must acknowledge that the natural forms the philosopher divides and combines are not merely an indiscriminate or undifferentiated herd. The eccentric quality of man and political life – which indicates the limits of "frozen" law and the impossibility of scientific statesmanship – points also to that "noetic heterogeneity" which precludes any doctrinaire metaphysics.[42] The whole remains elusive.[43]

Plato and Xenophon both seem to speculate, however, about what would be implied in the unnatural attempt to achieve complete "ruling" knowledge. The art of statesmanship involves trial and error, experience. It consists of giving commands. It might seem, then, that *complete* political knowledge can only be obtained through giving commands to all the beings that come within the statesman's art, i.e. the whole human race. (Would any biologist be satisfied with taxonomic knowledge that covered *most* mammals and *many* reptiles?) If there is an ontological parallel to the philosopher-king transcending the sovereignty of law, it might be the somewhat shocking idea of exercising tyranny over the Ideas. Could any greater erotic ambition be imagined? But what would this mean? Perhaps it would be sufficient to tyrannize over one Idea – the idea of man. But to rule the idea, the form itself, it would not be sufficient to rule merely some parts. Only a tyranny over the whole human species would consummate the theoretical mastery over an idea – the total assimilation of a natural form to a human art, a true philosophic *techne*.[44]

Because Socrates describes the Ideas as radically separate from the sensible world, we could see these speculations by Plato and Xenophon as fundamentally comical and anti-utopian. It becomes an interesting question, then, whether the Socratic ontology is more or less likely to open the door to political tyranny. I am not sure I agree with Waller Newell when he says that, for Plato, "the Forms, as the guide for philosophic and civic education, provided the best prospect for the rehabilitation of tyrannical aggression," but I do think Newell is correct that for Heidegger "the metaphysics of the Forms is *itself* the consummate attempt to tyrannize over the rest of existence, including human freedom."[45]

These abstruse reflections mainly serve to clarify – and here is the main point – the very dubious claims of any comprehensive political "science" which seeks to displace the moral virtue and practical wisdom of the statesman's prudence.

. . .

This brings us back, then, to the problem of Socrates and the essential question raised by his life and death: is all this discombobulating philosophical inquiry worthwhile? Can the philosopher justify his querulous prying and moral skepticism, which undermine the stability and good order of all regimes? Rather than taking these questions, or the answers, for granted, Harry Jaffa and his colleague Harry Neumann insisted that we give the most serious attention to the arguments – and divinations – *against* philosophy. We need to appreciate the moral-political integrity (and even the permanence) of the "closed city" with its overwhelming sense of civic piety. In the ancient world, these communities were radically undermined by Plato's new cosmopolitan "gods" of the transcendent Ideas. This never-closed question remains urgent both politically and philosophically.

As Neumann explains in one essay, the task of the philosopher nowadays is nearly the reverse of the challenge faced by

Socrates. Today, our blind spots come not from ossified ancient customs but from free-wheeling "humanistic or scientific education." What philosophers need now is "to secure a fair hearing for civic piety within their society."[46] In other words, Socrates's fellow Athenians simply assumed philosophy was bad. It is just as lazy and superficial, however, for us moderns to assume that philosophy is *good*.

CHAPTER III

THE ALTAR OF OUR FATHERS

The role of the gods in the classical world – not Plato's Ideas, but the potent, living gods for whom men killed and died – is explained masterfully in *The Ancient City*, by Denis Numa Fustel de Coulanges. As Fustel de Coulanges relates, in the ancient nations or city-states,[1] "religion intervened in all acts. It was everywhere present, it enveloped man." In Jerusalem, no less than Athens, or Sparta, or Carthage, "the soul, the body, private life, public life, meals, festivals, assemblies, tribunals, battles, all were under the empire of this city religion. It regulated all the acts of man, disposed of every instant of his life, fixed all his habits. It governed a human being with an authority so absolute that there was nothing beyond its control."[2]

As the gods kept each city together internally, the same divine authorities also kept the cities apart from each other:

> If we wished to give an exact definition of a citizen, we should say that it was a man who had the religion of the city. The stranger, on the contrary, is one who has not access to the worship, one whom the gods of the city do not protect, and who has not even the right to invoke them. For these national gods do not wish to receive prayers and offering except from citizens; they repulse the stranger;

entrance into their temples is forbidden to him, and his presence during the sacrifice is a sacrilege....

Thus religion established between the citizen and the stranger a profound and ineffaceable distinction. This same religion, so long as it held its sway over the minds of men, forbade the right of citizenship to be granted to a stranger....

No one could become a citizen at Athens if he was a citizen in another city; for it was a religious impossibility to be at the same time a member of two cities, as it also was to be a member of two families. One could not have two religions at the same time.[3]

Not only was there no conception whatsoever of religious liberty, even peaceful co-existence of separate tribes, and thus separate faiths, was difficult. Most ancient communities were united by ties of blood, since there was relatively little immigration. (Rome became in some sense the exception that proved this rule.) But they also regarded their gods as the original founders of their city. Patriotism – devotion to the *pater* (father) – meant ultimately devotion to the first father: the divine founder.

When cities went to war, their gods went to war. Thus, to conquer an enemy meant to obliterate his divinities:

Victory might make slaves of all the inhabitants of a conquered city, but they could not be made citizens of the victorious city. To join two cities in a single state, to unite the conquered population with the victors, and associate them under the same government... was never seen among the ancients....[4]

The spirit of the closed city, with its intense religious and civic comradery, seems to be deeply embedded in the human psyche.

Aristotle, who was familiar with various forms of government in the Mediterranean world, thought the *polis*, with about five thousand adult male citizens (along with women, children, and slaves) was the most natural form of political life – large enough for self-sufficiency but small enough to maintain a cohesive identity. Part of what we are seeing in the re-emerging tribalism of both Left and Right may be a reaction to the profound emptiness in the soul created by the loss of this "belonging," an attempt to recover a sense of meaning and purpose by recreating a holy community of citizen-believers.

If this is correct, it would help explain why the woke faithful show very little interest in talking to or persuading their deplorable opponents, but seem intent only on punitive domination. Again, Fustel de Coulanges seems to capture this spirit with uncanny accuracy: "There is no mercy for the enemy; war is implacable; religion presides over the struggle, and excites the combatants... they are permitted to kill the prisoners and the wounded." Absent any cosmopolitan idea of "the rights of man," there was nothing like the Geneva Convention. "Even outside the field of battle they have no idea of a duty of any kind towards the enemy. There are never any rights for a foreigner, least of all in time of war. No one was required to distinguish the just from the unjust...." [5]

If there is indeed a deep human need for these ancient ties of belief and belonging – a need radically suppressed by today's hedonistic secularism – then more of the mist obscuring our "cold civil war" may dissipate. When psychologists and sociologists speak of *alienation* and *existential angst* it is this spiritual emptiness to which they are referring – though most do not appreciate that it is essentially *political*. [6]

NEW MODES AND ORDERS

By the early 16th century, when Niccolò Machiavelli surveyed the political and philosophic scene in his home city of Florence as well as the rest of Christendom, the picture he beheld was bleak. Plato's abstract, trans-political ideas of universal justice had been integrated into Christian theology. When the Roman empire became Christian it obliterated all the ancient cities, along with their devotion to local and particular gods. Europe now included many earthly kingdoms but had only one faith – which created a kind of schizophrenia, dividing citizenship from piety.

Additionally, the status of philosophy had fallen into its own quandaries. The purely rational inquiry into questions of justice, the nature of being, and the order of the cosmos had been subsumed into theology, and thus mingled with the creeds of revelation. Philosophy/theology was still the preserve of the few, but Plato's caste of wealthy, leisured, and politically minded aristocrats had been replaced by friars and priests.

Strauss regarded Machiavelli as *the* philosopher who created a new world, the modern world, by launching a breathtakingly ambitious plan to fix both the political and the philosophic problems of Christian Europe. Christianity, Machiavelli believed, had rendered princes too weak and yet too fanatical, more concerned with eternal salvation than with effective governance. Whatever its ironic intentions, Plato's *Republic* offered a tantalizing account, "in speech," of a perfectly just regime ruled by the wise – a striking parallel to the "City of God" described by St. Augustine. Although in both theologies the Word describes a heavenly vision beyond our mortal reach, Platonic and Christian ideals fueled in some fanatic souls a passionate desire to create paradise on earth. The actual practice of Socratic philosophy, meanwhile, had ceased to be a means of elevating and enlarging the souls of ambitious young aristocrats, and had ossified into dogmas tended by cloistered monks.

In *Natural Right and History* (1953), Strauss outlines how the modern project refounded politics on a "low but solid" ground and invented a dramatic new role for science: to conquer nature for the relief of man's estate. Machiavelli, Strauss writes,

> rejected classical political philosophy, and therewith the whole tradition of political philosophy in the full sense of the term, as useless: classical political philosophy had taken its bearings by how man ought to live; the correct way of answering the question of the right order of society consists in taking one's bearings by how men actually do live. Machiavelli's "realistic" revolt against tradition led to the substitution of patriotism or merely political virtue for human excellence or, more particularly, for moral virtue and the contemplative life. It entailed a deliberate lowering of the ultimate goal. The goal was lowered in order to increase the probability of its attainment. Just as Hobbes later on abandoned the original meaning of wisdom in order to guarantee the actualization of wisdom, Machiavelli abandoned the original meaning of the good society or of the good life. What would happen to those natural inclinations of man or of the human soul whose demands simply transcended the lowered goal was of no concern to Machiavelli. He disregarded those inclinations. He limited his horizon in order to get results. And as for the power of chance, Fortuna appeared to him in the shape of a woman who can be forced by the right kind of men: chance can be conquered.[7]

That summary offers only a hint of what Strauss elsewhere called Machiavelli's "graceful, subtle, and colorful" teaching. For our purposes, it is sufficient to note that by various twists and turns this first wave became increasingly radical through the unfolding of modern philosophy, and it ultimately devolved into the radical atheism, scientism, and spiritual alienation we confront today. As Strauss explains in his "Three Waves" essay, Machiavelli's attempt to refound the basis of politics (and reclaim philosophy from the Church) entailed a rejection of both Christianity and classical rationalism. Yet this produced problems of its own, and each subsequent "wave" only exacerbated the problem by further radicalizing the premises implicit in Machiavelli's stupendous effort.

What was ultimately and most crucially lost was the classical conception of *nature*: the conviction that there is a fixed and intelligible order in the cosmos, outside of our will, that supplies a permanent ground of morality and justice. In the absence of nature, *history* and *science* became the authoritative substitutes. History would supply man's purpose by situating him within the course of historical progress. But this historicism teaches that we are not only situated but in fact *isolated* in our particular historic moment. Science, meanwhile, through its technical methodology, was intended to confirm man's mastery over the raw materials of nature, including human nature. Only that which can be counted and measured is real, and the only real knowledge is the quantifiable. (Contrast this with Plato's view in the *Statesman*, discussed above.)

Neither Science nor History, needless to say, has delivered on the promised results. As political scientist John Marini explains:

By recreating man as a historical being, his meaning is established in becoming.... That required a rejection of being and truth, or the eternal, as providing the necessary conditions, and limitations, on human understanding derived from philosophy and religion, and undermined the authority of nature, reason, and God. History dominated the mind of the intellectuals in the 19th century. But Nietzsche showed even before the end of that century that although History had undermined the authority of philosophy and religion and destroyed the human understanding of man in terms of nature or God, it could not establish the meaning of man in terms of the end of History or its rationality. History is irrational and never ending.[8]

Essentially egoistic and self-interested, concerned with nothing higher than his base appetites, modern man descends into what Gotthold Lessing called "the joyless quest for joy."

At the same time, science emerges as a tool of immense, almost uncontrollable, power. Martin Heidegger believed technological thinking had distorted the very essence of man's being. The modern project initiated by Machiavelli, glorifying man's ability to manipulate nature to serve our needs, leads ultimately to transforming the entire world, even human beings, into commodities to be processed. What science could *not* provide – what, in fact, was made exceedingly difficult – was a rational understanding of the human good.

One of the central themes of this book is this battle between the scientific-bureaucratic-rational state (which comes out of Hegel) and the post-modern rejection of all objective standards (which comes out of Nietzsche). Harry Neumann insisted that in this conflict the corrosive power of historicist nihilism will inevitably win out. This would mean, by the way, that in the factional struggle between the Left's oligarchic and anarchistic elements – Silicon Valley *versus* Antifa – the technocrats' wealth and power will eventually fail, since they have no solid basis on which to defend their legitimacy or expertise. Their trust in science is ultimately arbitrary. Neumann's judgment seemed to be shared by Leo Strauss, who showed that faith in the rational rule of intelligent experts could not withstand the Nietzschean critique. Anticipating Foucault and others, Strauss describes historicism this way:

> (1) It abandons the distinction between facts and values, because every understanding, however theoretical, implies specific evaluations. (2) It denies the authoritative character of modern science, which appears as only one among the many forms of man's intellectual orientation in the world. (3) It refuses to regard the historical process as fundamentally progressive, or, more generally stated, as reasonable. (4) It denies the relevance of the evolutionist thesis by contending that the evolution of man out of nonman cannot make intelligible man's humanity.

Thus, Strauss concluded, "Positivism necessarily transforms itself into historicism."[9]

. . .

This excursus into the roots of the crisis of the West now brings us back to the present day. First, there is one important clarification about a matter I have passed over almost entirely, namely, the place of the American founding within the modern project, and its relationship to modern philosophy. It is sufficient here to mention the scholarship of Thomas West, which argues persuasively against the facile assumption that America must be "low" because it is modern.[10] West's refutation of that view is corroborated in a compelling passage by Jaffa:

> In the American Founding, comfortable self-preservation may be said to become the end of limited government. But it does not replace prayer or thought as ends or principles of human life. Nor does it replace prayer or thought as the transpolitical ends of the regime, served by government but not directed or controlled by government. Rather, by removing prayer and thought from political control, limited government emancipates political life, and therefore human life, from the oppression of those conflicts which arise as to which are the true thoughts and which are the true prayers. It is able to do so because – but only because – revelation and reason are able to substantially agree upon what morality is.... The priority of rights reflects the authority of that Creator whose endowment they represent and who demands respect for them. Our respect for the rights of others constitutes an essential element of our duty to God, our primary duty, and the duty antecedent to our rights.[11]

The question of how to understand America is intimately connected to the relevance of political philosophy for the concerns of citizens. Is Strauss's true teaching a strictly apolitical focus on theoretical and eternal questions? Too many Straussians appear to assume the very point in doubt. They don't seem to consider seriously the questionableness of philosophy, and instead simply take for granted the goodness or legitimacy of challenging the moral authority of their regime. As Thomas West explains, students who are taught that political questions are simply subordinate to and derivative from theory – and thus assume everything important about America can be found in Thomas Hobbes and John Locke – will disdain political concerns as either unworthy or irrelevant. They will

> never ascend to the central question of philosophy because they will not feel the inescapable primacy of the question of what is the right way of life. They may study philosophical books, and they may pride themselves on their philosophic openness to all the serious questions. But when they take up works of political philosophy, they will view those works in a detached way, aesthetically, so to speak, as though they were working on an elegant sort of crossword puzzle or mathematical game. The ultimate consequence of a public critique of morality is the same as the effect of contemporary liberalism in academic life, namely to eviscerate philosophy by turning it into an easygoing moral relativism presided over by various in-groups of cognoscenti who applaud each others' refined interpretations of great books and ideas while they live the quite ordinary life of liberal intellectuals.[12]

FOUCAULT

This reference to the "ordinary life of liberal intellectuals" and their "easygoing moral relativism" seems anodyne; yet that life entails its own difficulties.

West's pungent comment invites us to wonder, what does

official or legitimate social science look like in an American regime caught between Hegel and Nietzsche? In much of academia, we continue to see the dominance of the postmodernism developed in the 20th century by diverse writers such as Jacques Derrida, Michel Foucault, Jacques Lacan, and Jean-Francois Lyotard. I want to focus on Foucault in particular and examine some of his writings that remain surprisingly useful for understanding the strange environment in which we now find ourselves. It might seem odd to reach back several decades to find the most incisive intellectuals for explaining the current state of social science. Yet if my earlier theory is correct – that America's culture war was put on hold for a quarter century – then it would make sense that these figures from the 1980s might still be relevant.

Foucault's central theme was the power discourse, or the relationship between political power, knowledge, and truth – though his conclusions are rather different from what Plato suggests in his treatment of the same themes in the *Statesman*. In one key essay Foucault writes:

> We are subjected to the production of truth through power and we cannot exercise power except through the production of truth.... I would say that we are forced to produce the truth of power that our society demands, of which it has need, in order to function: we *must* speak the truth; we are constrained or condemned to confess, or to discover the truth. Power never ceases its interrogation, its inquisition, its registration of truth: it institutionalizes, professionalizes, and rewards its pursuit. In the last analysis, we must produce truth as we must produce wealth, indeed, we must produce truth in order to produce wealth in the first place. (Emphasis by Foucault)[13]

Foucault, following Nietzsche in certain key respects, is saying that political power *produces* truth, and this projection of truth subsumes all the participants in that society. Foucault describes all those who accept the power dynamic as "willing subjects," who are completely implicated in and even defined by the official discourse. Their identity and outlook are established by the power structure. For example, the status granted by certain credentials, such as an Ivy League degree, is inseparable from the regime's overall legitimacy – which helps to explain how so many "respectable" people get coopted. In myriad ways, the subjugated individuals are constantly reenforcing the power structure by affirming their own identities. Although Foucault argues that this dynamic operates with greater intensity today, he believes it "is the case for every society." Truth, to reiterate, has no other standard, or ground, or mode of existence other than what is determined by the political power structure.

It might be tempting simply to dismiss this claim out of hand – as it was by many conservatives in the 1980s and '90s – as so much academic babble. But I would argue that we should reflect on Foucault's argument in part because he is offering a quite accurate description of how today's intellectuals perceive the world, and therefore how the ruling class, at least to some degree, thinks and operates. That's important to understand. Even if Foucault is wrong in his historicist or Nietzschean belief that these power structures define every society, it does seem to be the case for our society, *as far as our elites are concerned.* We would do well, therefore, to think through what this analysis means.

Moreover, despite some occasionally opaque jargon, Foucault's analyses often capture subtleties that others miss. For example, whereas many commentators today complain about official censorship, Foucault shows that power discourses often work in other, more indirect ways:

> There is no binary division to be made between what one says and what one does not say; we must try to determine the different ways of not saying such things, how those who can and those who cannot speak of them are distributed, which type of discourse is authorized, or which form of discretion is required in either case. There is not one but many silences, and they are an integral part of the strategies that underlie and permeate discourses.[14]

Altering the terms of "discretion," applying different pressures to produce different kinds of silence – that's not quite censorship, but it is a form of control. What other "strategies" does he mean? A large theme in Foucault's work is how power dynamics altered attitudes regarding sex.

> Rather than the uniform concern to hide sex, rather than a general prudishness of language, what distinguishes these last three centuries is the variety, the wide dispersion of devices that were invented for speaking about it, for having it be spoken about, for inducing it to speak of itself, for listening, recording, transcribing, and redistributing what is said about it: around sex, a whole network of varying, specific, and coercive transpositions into discourse. Rather than a massive censorship, beginning with the verbal proprieties imposed by the Age of Reason, what was involved was a regulated and polymorphous incitement to discourse.[15]

Some readers may find this language too impenetrable to take seriously. But Foucault is simply saying that by making sex something clinical and public – an object of regularized inspection, measurement, and deliberation – our whole conceptual framework shifts. To take only one obvious example, very few people nowadays are embarrassed to speak openly about matters that were once considered extremely private. Or think about what has happened to the word *unnatural* in regard to sexual activity. In terms of the contentious public debate now under way about trans rights, don't those who establish the terms of this "polymorphous incitement to discourse" exert a very potent form of control? Recall that Supreme Court Justice Ketanji Brown Jackson declared during her Senate confirmation hearing that she could not define the difference between a man and woman. What does this mean for her ability to distinguish a man from an animal, and thus adjudicate questions of human equality and natural rights?[16] It seems like Foucault does have something to teach about the connection between discourse and power.

In the fully developed bureaucratic state, the regime's rational structures pervade everything; the distinction between public and private breaks down. Therefore, the application of what Foucault called "biopower" replaces the governing of citizens with the regulation of populations. (This concept of biopower – sometimes called the biosecurity state – has been more recently taken up by Giorgio Agamben in his analysis of the COVID lockdowns as examples of Carl Schmitt's "state of exception."[17]) In theory, or ideally, the whole species of human organisms would be under unified control – i.e., globalism. This deployment of large-scale power means creating standards for and enforcing compliance with an established "norm."[18] (Recall Seth Benardete's observation, quoted above, that "the average suits everybody and fits nobody.") Winston Churchill already perceived this trend in the 1930s in an essay describing the suffocating "mass effects of modern life."

Reflecting on your own personal experiences living in the United States today, do you feel like a person, an individual human being, when you fly on a commercial airline or call customer service at a large company? Or do you feel more like a component in a mechanized process? Does it seem like anyone cares whether you, as an individual, are treated well – or even whether you are recognized as a person at all? Foucault helps us understand how we are now merely part of an aggregate. You can complain to these corporations, and your complaint will be logged and included with other complaints – as inputs to the system – and will be averaged out and entered into a formula for deciding whether the process should be changed. That's it. You are a unit in a complex mechanism which is meant to operate efficiently. Your time, and perhaps your convenience, might be factored into the equations governing how you are treated. But your dignity certainly has no quantitative value.

Foucault also shows that what may seem like propaganda and lies to abnormal or mentally recalcitrant[19] subjects are nothing but the ebb and flow of the power discourse as it modulates in response to environmental changes. These modulations and self-corrections are inherent to the bureaucratic regime – for the relatively minor reason that the experts' *hubris* requires them to deny their human fallibility, but more importantly because technical knowledge, as defined in any given moment, *is* the truth. That is one reason, incidentally, that no functionary in the administrative state is ever held personally responsible for anything. The *system* makes the decisions, though like any complex machinery it has occasional glitches.

Thus, in his famous "Discussion with Maoists" regarding

people's tribunals after a communist revolution, Foucault explains that notions of guilt, evidence, and neutrality are merely holdovers from the older power structure. A truly revolutionary form of justice would dispense with all that, in favor of simply recognizing that

> you have the masses and their enemies. Furthermore, the masses, when they perceive somebody to be an enemy, when they decide to punish this enemy – or to re-educate him – do not rely on an abstract universal idea of justice, they rely only on their own experience, that of the injuries they have suffered, that of the way in which they have been wronged, in which they have been oppressed; and finally, their decision is not an authoritative one, that is, they are not backed up by a state apparatus which has the power to enforce their decisions, they purely and simply carry them out.[20]

Neither "guilt" nor "truth" need wait upon procedures, especially since neither has any reality outside the discourse in any event; they are determined by the revolutionary cadres, the Party, the state, or whatever the power structure may be. This is why it is pointless to complain about the ruling class or regime media engaging in "hypocrisy." That is a meaningless charge which simply reflects a lingering attachment to various outmoded concepts (e.g. bourgeois logic, equal protection of the laws) that may have been upheld by the previous power structure, but which have now been displaced. Since the French Maoists that Foucault debated in 1971 had a hard time grasping this, it's not surprising that many Americans find it equally bewildering.

Emphasizing the often unseen yet comprehensive quality

of what Foucault sometimes called "governmentality," Rainer Friedrich, a professor of literature and classics, observes:

> No longer exercised by a sovereign, a ruling class, an oppressive state, or the military, modern power as power-knowledge is hidden in the institutional systems of modern society. It operates in the forms of the legal, administrative, educational, penal, scientific, medical, and psychiatric systems....[21]

Friedrich expresses some amazement that Foucault "detects and identifies power and 'effects of power' behind every bush: one wonders what is not power or an effect of power." But I don't find this surprising at all. There has to be some kind of substratum or ontological floor to human life, a canvas on which pious opinions or postmodern discourses express themselves and find their footing – however mysterious, in the case of Plato, or absurd, in the case of the postmodernists, this ground may be. In the absence of nature (abolished) and God (murdered) why not power? For us moderns, that seems at least as plausible as anything else. Friedrich is correct in seeing the dismal implications: "Being ubiquitous, omnipresent, omnipotent, and all-encompassing, power is inescapable: by stepping out from one set of power relations, one enters another one. No exit."

SPACES OF DOMINATION

For readers who still find Foucault's analyses too abstract, it may be helpful to note that many of his conclusions are corroborated by the very respectable, even dry, discipline of public administration. This topic is worth a brief detour, inasmuch as it helps to reveal some of the implications of these philosophical investigations.

John Marini observes that in the 21st century, "those who establish the meaning and method of the managerial class cannot even describe the state, and with good reason. They now call it the 'hollow state,' perhaps because they realize there is nothing there to define it." In the original conception of the rational state, as described by theorists such as Max Weber, "bureaucracy utilized instrumental reason on behalf of public purposes. There was a clear line between the public and private." Today, reason no longer holds sway, and what "has replaced the rational state is network analysis, which is a process and not an entity."[22]

Confirming this observation, a paper by Laurence O'Toole titled "The Implications for Democracy in a Networked Bureaucratic World," appearing in *the Journal of Public Administration Research and Theory*, describes present-day government bureaucracy as a series of elaborate networks that include

> interagency cooperative ventures; intergovernmental program management structures; complex contracting arrays; and public-private partnerships. They also include service-delivery systems reliant on clusters of providers that may include public agencies, business firms, not-for-profits, or even volunteer-staffed units, all linked by interdependence and some shared program interests.

The question that immediately arises in a constitutional republic is, who is accountable here? How do the people assert their sovereignty and exercise self-government when it isn't clear who is in charge, or when no one is really in charge? O'Toole notes that these networks "encourage a distancing of individuals from a sense that they themselves are acting [as well as an] objectification of those being dealt with." He observes laconically that "ethics may sometimes point in one direction, while concerns rooted in political obligation may suggest another."[23]

Hannah Arendt perceptively saw this as early as 1969, writing in the *New York Review of Books*, "In a fully developed bureaucracy there is nobody left with whom one could argue, to whom one could present grievances, on whom the pressures of power could be exerted. Bureaucracy is the form of government in which everybody is deprived of political freedom... for the rule by Nobody is not no-rule, and where all are equally powerless we have a tyranny without a tyrant."[24]

Writing in *Administration & Society* in 2005, Larry D. Terry's study on "The Thinning of Administration Institutions in the Hollow State" argues that attempts to apply business models to government bureaucracies and implement public-private networks do not in fact promote improved governmental performance but rather a declining "capacity for good administration." His analysis leads him to question "the long-term stability of the U.S. constitutional democracy" in light of these developments.[25] Rather than bringing the efficiencies of the private sector to government administration, the emergence of the hollow state and its bureaucratic networks have merely created mechanisms that attempt to solve problems that the networks themselves create and define. Marini echoes the work of Giorgio Agamben when he asks, "Was it the NIH (Fauci) that mandated the solution to COVID or was it the collaboration with Pfizer and the pharmaceutical companies that reached a mutually agreeable accommodation, enforced by political executives?"[26]

A paper published in 2007 by Arthur Sementeilli, with the foreboding title "Authority, Domination, and the Administrative State," discusses how "the loss of reason in our understanding of authority also portends a loss of discretion, individuality, and freedom." Developments in bureaucratic government have led to public authority being "denatured" and detached "from its grounding in traditional, legally and constitutionally empowered roles." Demonstrating the mainstreaming of postmodern thought, Sementelli observes that "authority in contemporary society has shifted from its roots in positivism, logic, and rationalism, toward one grounded in symbols and language games." Consistent with Foucault's argument that power never disappears but merely takes on new narrative forms, this study observes that modern structures of authority still rely on "some law, religious text, or social contract" which enable "their capacity to enforce rules and decisions." Importantly, however, "the nature of authority changes as a response to the *absence* of reason," and thus it becomes "increasingly difficult to separate ideology from policy." Modern trends in bureaucratic government reveal "how authority can become unhinged from reason and rationality, enabling spaces for domination."[27]

. . .

At this point we have to confront a somewhat tricky question, which can't be fully fleshed out in this short book. I claimed earlier that Plato and Foucault come to very different conclusions. But don't the power structures described by Foucault and these public administration scholars seem very similar to the *Republic*'s image of the cave? What is the difference between our regime's official narrative or discourse, and the ancient city's sacred customs and laws, the *nomoi* that regulate thought and behavior?[28] After all, Plato also insists that these authoritative myths provide the indispensable moral and theological sanction to law and opinion at all times in all caves. No exit. (At least no simple exit for us non-philosophic mortals.)

Strauss addresses this knotty question of knowledge and truth in a session of his 1957 course on the *Republic*:

> The contention of philosophy is that philosophy is possible. Philosophy means or is the attempt to replace opinions about this whole with knowledge of the whole. Is this attempt not absurd? The attempt of philosophy presupposes that the whole is intelligible and that the whole *is*.... How does Plato try to establish the basic premise of philosophy? Maybe this basic premise of philosophy has to be reformulated in accordance with what Plato actually does. In the crucial passage it is said only what is can be known. Moreover, it is clear that what is not cannot be known. This is the beginning.

What is can be known and what isn't can't. That doesn't seem like a very satisfying answer. Indeed, Strauss acknowledges, "what we have been discussing constitutes the most important difficulty in present-day thought in understanding Plato and Aristotle."

He goes on to address the paradox of the present-day solution, which asserts the impossibility of knowing the natural world and simultaneously claims perfect knowability of what is true and right. The way it does so bears a striking parallel to the modern project launched by Machiavelli and Hobbes: by lowering the ends of politics to the needs of the body a complete quantitative system of government could be established. Likewise, by reducing the knowable to our own mental constructs, the epistemological problem is solved by condensing reality to fit our minds. In both cases, the Gordian knot is cut by asserting our mastery over the world through an act of creation or will.

This, Strauss says, "leaves much to be desired." Modern reductionism simply tosses out what is hard to know and declares that "thought is essentially dependent on something non-thinking" (e.g. Marx's dialectical materialism or psychological behavioralism) which is "certainly at the opposite pole from what Plato and Aristotle thought."[29]

Strauss returns to these questions in the following seminar and offers a somewhat less fragmented answer, which shows that the problem of knowledge is already present in Kant. In response to the view that all thought is culturally bound, he says that the "frame of reference of a Tahitian is entirely different from that of someone else. These frames of reference thus have something arbitrary." Strauss seems to be referring to the variety of conventional opinions about justice and truth which led Socrates to wonder if there is anything right by nature. In order to replace opinion with knowledge, we need "a frame of reference which in principle can be common to all men as men." Strauss continues:

> Now there are two ways of conceiving this natural frame of reference, if I may call it this for the moment. One is the Kantian way, the other the Platonic way. Kant says there is a natural frame of reference which is given by the structure of the human mind. This implies that distinction

between the thing in itself and the phenomenon. This whole perception or understanding through this natural frame of reference is relative to man. The Platonic assertion is the opposite. This natural frame of reference is identical with the inner order of the whole.

What I understand Strauss to be saying is that reality either exists independently and it is our minds that must conform that objective reality (Plato), or whatever order or structure we may perceive in reality is actually *imposed* by the human mind (Kant). For Plato and the other Socratic philosophers, the truth is out there, so to speak, even if we can't grasp it completely. "We are by nature aware dimly of the essential structure of the whole," as Strauss explains.

This is expressed by Plato figuratively by the statement that we all have seen this essential order of the whole prior to our birth. This is the mythical formulation and not meant literally. What Plato regards as a matter of fact is that we do have such an awareness of the essential structure of the whole. In other words, there exists an essential kinship between the human mind and the essential, true structure of the whole.[30]

Classical political philosophy presupposes, though cannot prove apodictically, that the universe is intelligible.[31] We cannot reject with certainty Descartes's *Deus deceptor* (a hypothetical malicious demon who keeps us trapped in a world of random illusions). Or to take an example from popular culture, we cannot prove that we are not living in a computer simulation such as "The Matrix." We have to presume we are not sleepwalking. As a practical matter, the alternative to accepting the evident truth of our senses would seem to be moral and intellectual paralysis – or absurdity.[32]

Foucault acknowledged the hopelessness of his postmodern perspective, from which he saw no escape: "The relationship between rationalization and the excesses of political power is evident," he wrote. "And we should not need to wait for bureaucracy or concentration camps to recognize the existence of such relations." Yet, he asked, "what to do with such an evident fact? Shall we 'try' reason? To my mind, nothing would be more sterile." We are, he believed, "trapped in our own history."[33] For all his insights, Foucault could not see beyond the modern or postmodern horizon.

As Stanley Rosen explains, Foucault's arguments collapse on themselves. His

> disinterested or scientific study of power contradicts the passionate commitment of the left; the intention to liberate subjugated knowledges contradicts both scientific objectivity and the subjugating impulse of power politics.

Foucault is, Rosen concludes, "a postphilosopher and posthumanist connoisseur of subjugated discourses, not a philosopher at all."[34]

CHAPTER IV

PROGRESS OR THE RETURN
TO NATURE

MARTIN HEIDEGGER (Foucault's main teacher[1]) argued in the mid-20th century that modernity can go no further – that metaphysics as well as philosophy had come to an end; mankind can only "await new gods." Virtually no intellectual today would dispute this, or could even conceive of a coherent objection. Leo Strauss, however, seemed to think otherwise. What made him so different from other 20th-century thinkers? Strauss argued that classical, as opposed to modern, political philosophy begins with our prescientific experience of the common-sense world. "Classical political philosophy," he explained, "attempted to reach its goal by accepting the basic distinctions made in political life exactly in the sense and with the orientation in which they are made in political life, and by thinking them through, by understanding them as perfectly as possible.... It followed carefully and even scrupulously the articulation which is inherent in, and natural to, political life and its objectives."[2]

It may be precisely our recognition of being manipulated, as mentioned in the opening sentence of this book, that is getting in the way. Our cynical hyper-awareness of being "in the cave," our postmodern sophistication, actually drives us deeper underground and away from the natural experiences of moral-political life. We accept the idea of the authoritative political narrative or discourse, and then assume (as Foucault did) that reality is nothing *but* discourse.[3]

But Strauss argues that true "political understanding or political science cannot start from seeing the city as the cave but it must start from seeing the city as a world, as the highest in the world ...."[4] It may be for this reason that Strauss in class sometimes warned his students about being "too sophisticated." This can be taken, in some respects, as a defense of Jaffa, who was sometimes derided for being insufficiently aloof from political life and too engaged in moral hectoring. Professor Scot Zentner argues that Jaffa attempted to follow Strauss's advice by understanding the American regime with the piety of a citizen. As Zentner notes, Jaffa does not start from seeing the city as the cave, but (quoting Strauss) by "seeing man as completely immersed in political life."[5]

Moreover, Jaffa seemed to think that this classical or pre-scientific orientation was also at the heart of Strauss's own perspective. Interestingly, this view is corroborated by Professor Xiaofeng Liu. In quoting him earlier, I omitted the conclusion of his remarks on Strauss's project. Here it is:

> In general, it is agreed that Strauss's major preoccupations include the relationship between philosophy and theological politics, that between revelation and reason, and the quarrel between the ancients and the moderns. It is true that these were all preoccupations of his, but I think none of them is as pointed as this one: Strauss is primarily concerned with the moral degeneration of the philosopher. Strauss never denies Machiavelli's intellectual brilliance,

namely, "the intrepidity of his thought, the grandeur of his vision, and the graceful subtlety of his speech." But Strauss wants us to remember the "profound theological truth that the devil is a fallen angel." That is why in Machiavelli's thought there is "perverted nobility of a very high order."

"In my opinion," Liu reiterates, "the uniqueness of Strauss's way of reading is to be acutely attentive to the philosopher's moral-political quality, or the moral-political aspect of philosophy. This is the primary question of political philosophy." That is an extraordinary statement, which has passed – as far as I can tell – completely without notice or comment since it was published in *Interpretation*, the semi-official Straussian journal, seven years ago.

. . .

What [Gottfried] Benn called the West exists in a fragile, perhaps impossible, balance, and ever-endangered tension between freedom and slavery. Man's political cravings always are terrified by the West's scientific heart. Thus the more politically committed a nation becomes, the less western it is.
Harry Neumann[6]

Aristotle makes two emphatic statements about human nature that pull together the themes of this book. In his *Politics* and *Nicomachean Ethics* he says that man is by nature a political being (*zoon politikon*). At the beginning of the *Metaphysics* and in *De Anima* he asserts that all men desire to know. These two aspects of human nature, and the problems they bring with them, reveal themselves in countless ways wherever men are found. This is indeed what we would expect if historicism is false, and wisdom about the human condition still allows for the investigation of "the permanent questions."

The modern project to conquer nature is ultimately impossible, Harry Jaffa believed, for the reason cited by the Roman poet Horace: "although nature may be expelled with a pitchfork, it will always return." The contemporary return of tribalism, the reaction against the spiritual emptiness of modern life, is proof that that man's political nature can be suppressed but never destroyed. If this is to be a cause of hope, however, it will only be if this yearning finds some purpose beyond passionate fighting and animal desire. The brute instincts rebelling against mankind's technical commodification must be guided by that other aspect of human nature: the desire to know.

The primal urge to believe and belong seems to be erupting in such alarming ways because it is expressing itself only in resentment and racial antagonism. To become properly political, to establish the conditions for a virtuous life, those instincts must be elevated by rational thought. If our moral-political divide leads only to a battle of wills and preferences, it would be no more dignified or meaningful than scorpions fighting in a bottle.

In his course on Plato's *Apology* and *Crito*, Strauss comments on this intellectually flattening effect of modern ideologies:

> Now despite the almost overwhelming power of positivism and historicism in our age, the simple reasoning leading up to political philosophy – a reasoning which I sketched – has not lost its primary evidence, and therefore we see time and again people, also young people, rebel more or less strongly against this value-free or valueless conception of

social science. But this primary evidence doubtless needs now some external support against this terrific *steamroller*, which [threatens] to bury everything else. And that, I think, is the reason why it is a good thought to study Plato: in order to clarify and to strengthen the primary evidence in favor of the concern with the good society.

We may wonder if one purpose, perhaps the main purpose, of Strauss's scholarship was to help us do just that.

.   .   .

Giorgio Agamben solemnly concludes his book *Where are We Now: The Epidemic as Politics* by claiming that the world begun with the Industrial Revolution is ending:

> We do not regret the ending of this world. We have no nostalgia for the notions of the human and of the divine that the implacable waves of time are erasing from the shore of history. But we reject with equal conviction the mute and faceless bare life and the health religion that governments are proposing. We are not awaiting either a new God or a new human being. We rather seek, here and now, among the ruins around us, a humbler, simpler form of life. We know that such a life is not a mirage, because we have memories and experiences of it – even if, inside and outside of ourselves, opposing forces are always pushing it back into oblivion.[7]

Agamben says no more than this. But I think that Strauss and Jaffa would not leave the matter there. What might their teaching suggest to us? Let me offer few a preliminary conclusions and pose several questions, which are not offered with the expectation of any immediate or definitive answers, but rather as matters deserving of further reflection.

HISTORY

Can Americans recover a meaningful appreciation for history in a way that provides us with a common purpose and identity? Overcoming encroaching Orwellianism, and repudiating the lies of the 1619 Project, while indispensable, would only be tactical victories absent a deeper understanding of how historicism or historical consciousness has distorted our approach to reality. Above all, does political philosophy still understand its own non-historicist preconditions?

In *On Tyranny*, Strauss warned of the possibility of a universal, homogenous state that could mean "the end of philosophy on earth." The preservation of philosophy, he argued, meant preserving or recovering the possibility of Socratic rationalism. But this was only possible, as he argued elsewhere, through a conception of history in which the

> fundamental problems, such as the problems of justice, persist or retain their identity in all historical change, however much they may be obscured by the temporary denial of their relevance and however variable or provisional all human solutions to these problems may be. In grasping these problems as problems, *the human mind liberates itself from its historical limitations.* No more is needed to legitimize philosophy in its original, Socratic

sense: philosophy is knowledge that one does not know; that is to say, it is knowledge of what one does not know, or awareness of the fundamental problems and, therewith, of the fundamental alternatives regarding their solution that are coeval with human thought. (Emphasis added)[8]

What are Strauss's students prepared to do *politically* to defend *philosophy* from the new enemies of reason, who repudiate both western civilization and the very possibility of transhistorical wisdom? Today's woke ideologues are not aristocratic dilettantes practicing a refined sophistry, but resolute militants on behalf of a primitive will to power. Are liberal Straussians prepared to call this barbarism by its rightful name? In 1948, Strauss expressed his disgust at the inability of modern social science to identify tyranny even when confronted with its most savage form. Have today's Straussians settled into their own irresponsible complacency? Have they forgotten or repudiated this lesson of Strauss's courageous defense of human freedom?

RELIGION

What role will religion play in the future? There are signs of an emerging paganism throughout the world.[9] Superstition, mysticism, gnosticism, and even less savory alternatives have filled man's spiritual needs in the past and may do so again. Yet it would perhaps be premature to say farewell to the Bible. In his despair over modern man's alienation from being and the loss of authentic life, Heidegger suggested that "the East," and specifically China, could offer Western civilization a path out of our desiccated condition. Without disparaging these other traditions, Strauss responded to this suggestion by arguing that we already have "the East within us" – in the form of the Bible.[10] If Strauss is right, this may prove to be a great salvation indeed, since China, so far from offering solutions from outside the Western tradition, seems to be turning to the West – and even specifically to Leo Strauss – for guidance in its own self-understanding. Some Chinese scholars seem to believe that although their ancient culture retains a connection to premodern traditions in the form of Confucianism, China has already, in key respects, been absorbed into the Western technical mode of being. Strauss's recovery of the classical confrontation between Athens and Jerusalem, they hope, can offer a way out of this dilemma.

It will matter very much, therefore, how we approach the Bible. As Jaffa often explained, both reason and revelation have become detached from moral-political life. Most mainline churches now operate wholly within the modern horizon. The Bible is no longer accessible to us as morally obedient people, as faithful people. We read it in the spirit of "criticism" – as a text. But merely resurrecting a literary or philological study of the Bible, or pursuing the "East within us" as an archeological expedition, is not sufficient.

Many disaffected young people on the Right see revelation as the most radical alternative to the spiritual emptiness of modernity, while many pleasant churchgoers accept the "stories" of the Bible as morally edifying. Yet one may wonder, in both cases, how these religious sentimentalists would regard the intense faith of pre-modern Christianity, which might seem to them as strange and repellant as the Romans' worship of their *lares* and *penates.*

Renewing the productive tension between reason and revelation can only take place by recovering the pre-scientific form of pious rootedness. What role can the faithful play in this endeavor in the absence of ecclesiastical leadership? What are the prospects for another Great Awakening, and what form would it take?

SCIENCE

The question of science is essentially the question of nature and whether we can restore a common-sense understanding of the natural world that overcomes the immense power of scientism or "technical rationality."

John Marini explains that for the Progressives of late 19th and early 20th century, "social intelligence" established the direction of progress, and thus represents the will of the people. Though the claims of technical rationality are becoming ever more hollow, the bureaucracy still operates on the presumption that its expertise transcends the consent of the governed. "It is not yet clear," Marini observes,

> what forces – intellectual, economic, social, and political – will establish the mastery of the modern world in the 21st century.... It remains to be seen if the American people understand or will come to understand themselves as political citizens of the nation-state, or as administrative subjects of a rational global order. Much depends upon whether the American people have become so dependent upon the administrative state that the overthrow of the established order is not merely difficult, but undesirable. In that case, political self-government, and individual freedom, will cease to be important elements of the American regime.[11]

Even if we are blessed with the emergence of a statesman who can challenge the political authority of the administrative state, can that be sufficient without arguments from the academic and scientific communities that counteract the theoretical dogmas occluding our thinking? What can be done to promote this scholarship and develop these arguments?

MORALITY

The American people are drowning in deceit and propaganda. The extent to which technology invades every space and moment of our lives means that our understanding of reality is manipulated to a far greater extent than was achieved by the former Soviet Union.[12] This might seem to be an observation more suitable under the heading of *Science* above. But it is the possibility of *morality* that is at stake in whether or not we can still comprehend what Strauss called "those simple experiences regarding right and wrong which are at the bottom of the philosophic contention that there is a natural right."

To restore healthy political life, indeed healthy *human* life, will require first and foremost recovering our access to nature or the natural world – by which I do not mean environmentalism or camping, but rather the moral reality that is or ought to be evident to common sense. Strauss explains this beautifully in his eulogy for Winston Churchill, delivered in class in 1965:

> The death of Churchill reminds us of the limitations of our craft, and therewith of our duty. We have no higher duty, and no more pressing duty, than to remind ourselves and our students, of political greatness, human greatness, of

the peaks of human excellence. For we are supposed to train ourselves and others in seeing things as they are, and this means above all in seeing their greatness and their misery, their excellence and their vileness, their nobility and their triumphs, and therefore never to mistake mediocrity, however brilliant, for true greatness.[13]

What Strauss describes can, and indeed must, be a work of political philosophy. But it cannot be *only* an effort by academic students of political philosophy. It is above all the work of citizens, of morally serious men and women, dedicated to recovering "our ancient faith." What can each of us do as individuals, as members of communities and congregations, and as citizens? Virtue, unlike "social intelligence," can only be cultivated one soul at a time.

What is perhaps most disconcerting about the anti-liberal elements of the Right is not the vehemence of their complaints against modernity, but their cynical retreat from politics, in the false belief that nothing can be done. Despair, Jaffa was fond of saying, is not only a sin (because it presumes we have been abandoned by God), but also an intellectual error. If historical determinism is false, it means that virtue and chance will always play a part in shaping our destinies, and that the choices we make in exercising our moral freedom can be decisive, even in ways we may not expect.

What Plato shows in the *Statesman* is that the true art of politics denies both the tyranny of perfect knowledge and the tyranny of perfect care – even or especially when they appear in the same guise. The genuine statesman attempts to rule neither as scientist nor shepherd, because as a famous American said, "Almighty God hath created the mind free." But the question of freedom points to another false choice: the alternative to oppressive bureaucracy is not irrational lawlessness. Between Hegel's total state and Nietzschean anarchy lies another choice: self-government. Man is ever the in-between creature.

HONORABLE AMBITION

In response to the question of whether political philosophy can really do anything to save Western civilization, Jaffa responded by asserting that such an effort can never be certain of success. Yet, in the fight for our civilization, "we have no reason to believe that we must fail. If we do not know that we must fail, we have a duty to persevere in our political efforts to reverse the decline of the West." Success or failure are secondary to whether we "have lived our lives well. For the heart of the enterprise of political philosophy lies in the distinction between vulgar success and noble failure."

> The destiny of the human soul does indeed lie in eternity, not in history. But the destiny of souls in eternity is reflected in how they act in history, in their moral and political lives in this world. Western civilization is above all... constituted by a concern for eternity, whether by the instruments of reason or of revelation.[14]

These beautiful words might seem to offer slender hope for meeting the *practical* crisis of our time. Indeed, Strauss, in a famous passage that appears to turn away from the primacy of the theoretical, says the hope against global tyranny lies in the fact that "there will always be men (*andres*) who will revolt against a state which is destructive of humanity or in which there is no longer a possibility of noble action and great deeds."[15] If he does not mean simply "resolute will," which in any case cannot properly regard itself as noble, we may recall that the man ambitious for honor is not necessarily closed to philosophy, and that "manliness and wisdom belong together."[16] The immoderate skepticism of Socratic *eros* remains the most moderate and promising alternative to our twin political dangers of rational tyranny and tribal passions, because in its original form as the awareness of ignorance that quest offers perhaps the most powerful and humanizing antidote to dogmatic certainty: wonder.

NOTES

INTRODUCTION

1   Seminar on Plato's *Gorgias*, session 1, January 3, 1957.

2   https://www.psychologytoday.com/us/blog/vitality/201205/
facebook-and-your-brain.

3   On an almost weekly basis – from Hunter Biden's laptop, to the changing
narrative on COVID, to the endless stream of racist hoaxes – the establishment's disinformation is promulgated, then debunked, then forgotten. But accepting official lies as normal is fatal to self-government, and
even opens the door to a kind of psychological suicide. Consider Hannah Arendt's observation in *Origins of Totalitarianism*:

> In an ever-changing, incomprehensible world the masses had
> reached the point where they would, at the same time, believe
> everything and nothing, think that everything was possible and that
> nothing was true. Mass propaganda discovered that its audience
> was ready at all times to believe the worst, no matter how absurd,
> and did not particularly object to being deceived because it held
> every statement to be a lie anyhow. The totalitarian mass leaders
> based their propaganda on the correct psychological assumption
> that, under such conditions, one could make people believe the
> most fantastic statements one day, and trust that if the next day they
> were given irrefutable proof of their falsehood, they would take ref-
> uge in cynicism; instead of deserting the leaders who had lied to
> them, they would protest that they had known all along that the
> statement was a lie and would admire the leaders for their superior
> tactical cleverness.

4   It's important to acknowledge that the current national security surveillance state is not only, or even primarily, a creation of the Left. Conservatives endorsed, over the years, a great deal of the federal authority
and institutional mechanisms now being used against them. This error,
though, can be explained and even justified by the need to fight Soviet
espionage and imperialism during the Cold War. That very fact seems

to be instructive confirmation of an observation by Leo Strauss regarding ancient versus modern philosophy:

> The classics were for almost all practical purposes what now are called conservatives. In contradistinction to many present-day conservatives however, they knew that one cannot be distrustful of political or social change without being distrustful of technological change.... Yet they were forced to make one crucial exception. They had to admit the necessity of encouraging inventions pertaining to the art of war. They had to bow to the necessity of defense or of resistance. This means however that they had to admit that the moral-political supervision of inventions by the good and wise city is necessarily limited by the need of adaptation to the practices of morally inferior cities which scorn such supervision because their end is acquisition or ease. They had to admit in other words that in an important respect the good has to take its bearings by the practice of bad cities or that the bad impose their law on the good.
>
> *Thoughts on Machiavelli*, 298–299.

Something like this phenomenon is what leads Carl Schmitt to define sovereignty as the one who decides the "state of exception" – that is, the one (often the chief executive) who has the authority to decide that exigent circumstances authorize the suspension of the constitution and the laws. (See chapter one of his *Political Theology*.)

CHAPTER I

1 The late Harry Jaffa has been, by far, my greatest influence. I came to appreciate his colleague, Harry Neumann, too late to learn more from him directly when I had the opportunity as a graduate student in Claremont in the 1990s. I am also indebted to many friends and teachers, especially Mike Anton, Mickey Craig, Ed Erler, Chris Flannery, Charles Kesler, John Marini, and Tom West.

2 Willmoore Kendall, *The Conservative Affirmation* (2022), 102. At the most extreme point of incompatibility, one or both factions will be incapable of comprehending any form of citizenship in which the "other" can participate, because those others exist in a different metaphysical category.

3 https://www.cbsnews.com/news/anthony-fauci-face-the-nation-transcript-11-27-2022/.

4   Nietzsche, *Genealogy of Morals*, trans. Douglas Smith, 30.
5   Ibid, 101.
6   Ibid, 106.
7   *Interpretation*, Spring 1999, passim.
8   Strauss, *Natural Right and History*, 2.
9   The only copy of the book available in English omits any information about the publisher, and also lacks page numbers.

CHAPTER II

1   Neumann, "The New Left and the Socratic Tradition: The Problem of Ancient Piety in Modern Politics," *Claremont Journal of Public Affairs*, 4, 1977.
2   Neumann, *Liberalism*, xi–xii.
3   Consider this remarkable account by a former student:

> "Remember our senior year," asks Loewen, "when Nixon bombed Cambodia and it was like there was no greater event in the history of mankind? And the faculty voted to close down all the campuses?" I remember. In fact, a group of us occupied the ROTC building and, in what we thought of as a delightful irony, spent the whole night playing Risk, the game of world conquest. "Well," continues Loewen, "there's something that has really stuck with me. There was a young philosophy professor at Scripps – he later moved to Claremont Graduate School – named Harry Neumann, who I heard was still holding class that day. He was jeopardizing his whole career doing this, taking the risk of being denied tenure, so a couple of us headed over there. It was a seminar on Nietzsche, and in addition to its nine or ten students, there were 40 or 50 others hanging around the walls of this little room. What he was discussing was indecipherable to me, but finally he looked up, acknowledging that all these other people were around. And he said: 'At the faculty meeting yesterday, somebody asked me when, if ever, I would close the university. And I told him: When all the answers to all the important questions have been found, then it would be appropriate to close the university. And for all the people who have all the answers to all the important questions, the university is already closed.'"

> Harry Stein, "How My Friends and I Wrecked Pomona College," *City Journal*, Spring 2016.

4   Gildin, ed., *An Introduction to Political Philosophy: Ten Essays by Leo Strauss*, 81–98.

5   Carey, Jackson, Antonello, and Rushing, "Glaciers, gender, and science: A feminist glaciology framework for global environmental change research," *Progress in Human Geography*, Volume 40, Issue 6, December 2016.

6   Quoted in Giorgio Agamben, *Homo Sacer*, 3.

7   Jaffa, *Crisis of the Strauss Divided*, 51.

8   Liu, "Leo Strauss and the Rebirth of Classics in China," *Interpretation*, Spring 2016.

9   Strauss, *Natural Right and History*, 93.

10 Neumann, "Atheistic Freedom and the International Society for the Suppression of Savage Custom: An Interpretation of Conrad's *Heart of Darkness*," *Interpretation*, Winter 1974.

11 Strauss, *What is Political Philosophy?*, 80–81.

12 It is hard not to commiserate with this turn to pre- or anti-modern martial spiritedness, and recognize that the racial elements in this vitalism are in some ways an understandable reaction to the ethnic-identity obsessions of the Left. But any life-affirming nobility and excellence grounded in man's biological reality (as opposed to, say, his intellectual or political nature) evades the essential problem, in much the same way that Nietzsche himself does. Strauss observes, "Man's creativity presupposes things which are not created by man. Man's very creativity is not created by man: it presupposes, as we say, nature. But how is this compatible with the claim raised on behalf of human creativity, the human will to power? Is it so that Nietzsche can understand nature only as willed, as a human postulate? Is it so that Nietzsche needs nature and yet cannot recognize it as nature? This is the question." Seminar on Nietzsche, 1967, session three, no date. See also *Leo Strauss on Nietzsche's* Thus Spoke Zarathustra, Richard Velkley ed., 139, 189–190.

13 Neumann, "Political Theology? An Interpretation of Genesis (3:5, 22)," *Interpretation*, Fall 1995.

14 "While it has by no means wholly lost its triumphal self-assurance Athens has suffered far greater losses than Pericles ever led it to suspect it would…. The Athens to which Socrates returns [in 429 B.C.] is a newly needy Athens faced with the existential crisis of the invading Spartans and the plague, but faced as well with a deep spiritual crisis generated

by the visible crises and recognizable in these earliest stages only by a person with the widest perspective and deepest insight...." Lawrence Lampert, *How Philosophy Became Socratic*, 147. Leo Strauss notes, "Classical political philosophy is non-traditional, because it belongs to the fertile moment when all political traditions were shaken...." *What is Political Philosophy*, 27. Nietzsche asserts that Socrates "saw *through* his noble Athenian; he comprehended that his own case, his idiosyncracy, was no longer exceptional. The same kind of degeneration was quietly developing everywhere: old Athens was coming to an end." *Twilight of the Idols*, "The Problem of Socrates," trans. Walter Kaufmann.

15 Jaffa, *Strauss Divided*, 136.

16 Rosen, *Plato's* Republic: *A Study*, 229–230. In the *Republic* (619b–c) and *Gorgias* (492b–d) Socrates suggests that all non-philosophers wish to be tyrants to satisfy the desires of their bodies. If philosophers have an equivalent desire to satisfy an intellectual *eros*, one might say that tyranny is a universal temptation.

17 However different in style, Strauss argued that Plato and Xenophon were very nearly identical in substance. On Xenophon's treatment of philosophic tyranny, see Thomas Pangle's perceptive observations in his commentary on the *Memorabilia*, where he remarks on the general "scholarly bewilderment at the idea that Socrates's dialogic art could be a crucial source of political power." Xenophon's Socrates suggests that skill in dialectic goes together with the art of the exemplary leader (*hegemonikōtatous*). Pangle notes that in the central passage of the *Hiero*, "Xenophon has a great tyrant disclose that tyrants have a fear of wise dialecticians, for their uncanny capacity to 'contrive something' [and] indicates his awareness that the poet, with such wisdom, could well succeed in replacing Hiero as the new tyrant." Pangle adds, "[c]onventional scholars have not reckoned with the political power entailed in the liberation from illusions, and in the profound understanding of human psychology – not least the psychology of the politically ambitious and hence of one's political rivals as well as of oneself – that is essential to authentic Socratic dialectical refutations." *The Socratic Way of Life: Xenophon's* Memorabilia, 227–228, n. 18.

18 Strauss, *On Tyranny*, 207.

19 *The Republic of Plato*, trans. Allan Bloom, 434.

20 Seminar on *Apology* and *Crito*, session 1, October 18, 1966. Consider also Strauss's remarks in another lecture:

The implication is this: regarding all parts of your welfare or well-being (or most of the parts), you have experts, but regarding your well-being and happiness as a whole, there are no experts. That everyone must do for himself. Now there are people who cannot take care of their well-being as a whole. Must they be sent to experts? Well, we always have such people around – I have forgotten the delicate and euphemistic term used, which is quite common. But think simply of children. Children cannot take care of their well-being as a whole: they have parents. Therefore a mature human being, if he is not truly (what is the term they use?) moronic, more or less must be able to take care of himself. That cannot be left to any experts. There is no expertise regarding ethics.

Introduction to Political Philosophy, session 15, March 10, 1965.

21 This has become something of a cliché in some circles. One analytic philosopher observes, "The animosity of analytical philosophy toward what I call 'vulgar Straussianism' is certainly well deserved; vulgar Straussians practice a reductive hermeneutics where all classical texts end up saying the same thing (i.e., something like Nietzschean nihilism is true and needs to be overcome, or – what amounts to the same – endorsed)." https://www.newappsblog.com/2013/08/on-leo-strauss-and-the-philosophers.html.

22 Jaffa, *American Conservatism and the American Founding*, 57.

23 Jaffa, *Crisis of the House Divided*, 50th anniversary edition, v.

24 Benardete, *Plato's Statesman*, 132.

25 In the *Charmides* (166e) moderation is defined very expansively as "knowledge both of itself and all other knowledges." (Trans. West) Ronna Burger observes that this "scientific" and "architectonic" knowledge is "espoused not by Socrates but by Critias, future member of the Thirty Tyrants, who has found in Socratic principles the promise of a justification for tyrannical political power." *Aristotle's Dialogue with Socrates*, 250–251.

26 Xenophon tells us in his *Symposium* (2.10) that Socrates married a difficult wife to experiment with the problem of dealing with people in general, and claims that "if I can endure her, I'll easily associate with all other human beings." In the end, Socrates failed to tame or educate the city, as he failed to tame or educate his wife. Philosophic tyranny is best confined to experiments in speech – a lesson some of Plato's readers may have missed.

27 Blitz, *Plato's Political Philosophy*, 241.

28 Strauss, *On Tyranny*, 278.

29 It is interesting to compare Strauss's language in his celebrated essay, "What is Political Philosophy?" which seems to reenforce the teaching of the *Statesman*:

> Men are constantly attracted and deluded by two opposite charms: the charm of competence which is engendered by mathematics and everything akin to mathematics, and the charm of humble awe, which is engendered by meditation on the human soul and its experiences. Philosophy is characterized by the gentle, if firm, refusal to succumb to either charm. It is the highest form of the mating of courage and moderation. In spite of its highness or nobility, it could appear as Sisyphean or ugly, when one contrasts its achievement with its goal. Yet it is necessarily accompanied, sustained, and elevated by eros. It is graced by nature's grace.

30 Benardete, *Plato's Statesman*, xiv.

31 In his translation of Farabi's *Philosophy of Plato and Aristotle*, Muhsin Mahdi remarks on the comparison of the philosopher and the prince in Farabi's commentary on the *Statesman*, "There is a persistent ambiguity throughout this section as to whether there is one or two skills and faculties." 142 n. 22.

32 Klein, *Plato's Trilogy: Theaetetus, the Sophist and the Statesman*, 172.

33 Foucault's analysis is worth quoting at some length:

> Only a god in a Golden Age could ever act like that.... [The] men who hold political power are not to be shepherds. Their task doesn't consist in fostering the life of a group of individuals. It consists in forming and assuring the city's unity. In short, the political problem is that of the relation between the one and the many in the framework of the city and its citizens. The pastoral problem concerns the lives of individuals. All this seems very remote, perhaps. The reason for my insisting on these ancient texts is that they show us how early this problem – or rather, this series of problems – arose. They span the entirety of Western history. They are still highly important for contemporary society. They deal with the relations between political power at work within the state as a legal framework of unity, and a power we can call "pastoral," whose role is to constantly ensure, sustain, and improve the lives of each and every one. The well-known "welfare state problem" does not only bring the needs

or the new governmental techniques of today's world to light. It must be recognized for what it is: one of the extremely numerous reappearances of the tricky adjustment between political power wielded over legal subjects and pastoral power wielded over live individuals.

"*Omnes et Singulatim*: Towards a Criticism of Political Reason,"
Tanner Lectures on Human Values, 1979.

34 Strauss, seminar on the *Gorgias*, session 15, March 10, 1957.

35 See, e.g., *Federalist Papers* 23, 34, 70, and 74.

36 Jaffa, *American Conservatism and the American Founding*, 34–35. In his latest book, *Liberalism and Its Discontents*, Francis Fukuyama criticizes an essay I wrote for *The American Mind* in 2021 because I fail to appreciate the diversity of those who reject the founders' republicanism. Fukuyama thinks the solution to our political crisis is for those on the Right to embrace diversity and "make use of it to support conservative values." See pages 118–119 and 145.

37 Benardete, *Plato's "Laws": The Discovery of Being*, 139ff. Consider especially the complex interaction of law and poetry in creating what Strauss called "divinations." (pp. 145–152)

38 Avicenna referred to Plato's *Laws* as "the treatment of prophecy and the Divine Law." See Strauss's *The Argument and the Action of Plato's Laws*, 1.

39 The greatest threat posed by both the philosopher and the tyrant – perhaps because both are shameless – may be to the ontological and theological foundation of the laws. For different reasons, tyrants and philosophers both challenge the defining conventions and sacred restraints of the regime. This undermines not only the citizens' pious belief in the divine authority of the laws, but even more importantly, the deeper understanding of man and his place in relation to nature and the gods. (See *Republic* 560d–e and 571c.) Bloom's interpretative essay in his *Republic* translation is helpful: "The need for overcoming shame becomes clear in relation to what Socrates considers to be another form of *eros* – intellectual or philosophic *eros*. Souls, in order to know, must strip away the conventions which cover their nature. Shame prevents them from doing this just as it prevents them from stripping their bodies." (p. 382) The power of the sacred seems to be expressed in shame; even Thrasymachus blushes (*Republic*, 350d). See Ronna Burger's "Definitional Law in the Bible," in *The Eccentric Core: The Thought of Seth Benardete*.

40 "It ought to be known that this is similar to a flight of stairs that one climbs up and another comes down; the distance is the same, although there is a difference between the two pursuits." Farabi, *The Harmonization of the Opinions of the Two Sages*, 4.21–22. Trans. Butterworth.

41 The "second sailing of the ideas was inseparable from the promotion by Socrates of the soul as a nonderivative principle. Ontology, epistemology, and psychology were thereby joined and hence transformed, and it was one of Strauss's most beautiful discoveries to put together logos, being, and soul." Benardete, *The Argument of the Action*, 410. Among the infinite questions one could still explore on this topic, I offer one that remains especially mysterious (at least to me): What is the ontological counterpart to the sacred, which provides compulsion to the laws? The political statesman, it seems, when altering laws after an absence, would be practically limited to modifications that do not greatly shock pious sensibilities. What divine aspects of being command similar deference from a metaphysical logos?

The difficult term *noetic heterogeneity* refers to an intelligible order of reality that seems to include natural divisions or types. In contrast to pre-Socratic doctrines of atomism or materialism – which usually reduced everything to a single element, such as water – this view holds that the cosmos includes a variety of different species or classes of things, which are many but not infinitely many. An infinity of different kinds would mean that each thing in the world is unique, which would make intelligible speech or thought impossible. Every individual dog may be special, yet we can still speak about dogs – as well as trees, chairs, and regimes – in general. If every being required its own unique name and could not be grouped into a class or species, then the universe would consist only of an endless series of proper nouns, again making speech or thought impossible. Noetic heterogeneity – i.e. natural kinds and thus common nouns – falls between homogenous sameness and infinite variety. (Jaffa was fond of speaking about "the miracle of the common noun." See for example his speech at Rosary College, available here: https://claremontreviewofbooks.com/a-conversation-with-harry-v-jaffa/.)

42 Strauss explains it this way in one lecture:

> The Platonic doctrine can now be stated as follows: the whole is characterized by non–sensible, by noetic [heterogeneity]. This is a characteristic Platonic thesis. These noetic heterogeneous elements of which the whole consists, these are the ideas. All later thought

has recognized, in one way or other, this Socratic statement. All later thought admits that the whole consists of essentially different parts. In other words, the question, "Out of what did the whole come into being?," cannot even be raised before you know the whole as it is, just as you cannot answer the question of who made this chair before you know the chair as chair. The essence of the whole is its intrinsic structure. You have to put this together with what I said last time about the idea[s] as classes of things and [as goals] of aspiration or as models. Then you will gradually reach a better understanding of what that means....

The principle of Platonic philosophy is that the whole, the nerve of the whole, is characterized [by] noetic heterogeneity. In other words, the whole essentially consists of parts and cannot be understood as homogeneous. Secondly, this heterogeneity has a noetic character. The essential difference between, say, plant and root, or between man and root, or between dog and cat – this cannot be understood in terms of their sensible qualities; grasping the essential difference is no longer sensible. For Plato, full knowledge is impossible. Since no idea is wholly independent of the other ideas, there is no possibility of complete knowledge of an idea without complete knowledge of the whole. You can say there is an iron wall which keeps the whole together.

Seminar on the *Gorgias*, Session 12, February 26, 1957.

43 In quantum mechanics, Heisenberg's Uncertainty Principle stipulates that it is impossible, even in theory, to capture simultaneously the velocity and the position of a subatomic particle. I wonder if this corroborates in some way the observation frequently made by Strauss that every Platonic dialogue abstracts from something essential. To capture one truth, it is necessary to let go of another.

44 While "condemnation of tyranny was certainly the majority viewpoint... this pervasive fear and hatred for tyranny was accompanied by an ambiguous fascination with unrestrained and absolute power. As we will see, we can find significant traces of this fascination in Thucydides and Aristophanes, as well as in the idea of the happiness of the tyrant, attributed to Polus, Callicles, and Thrasymachus in Plato's *Gorgias* and *Republic*, and of which we find an echo in Xenophon's *Hiero*." Cinzia Arruzza, *A Wolf in the City: Tyranny and the Tyrant in Plato's*

Republic, 32. It is interesting to consider how the early theorists of public administration, who trace their roots to Hegel, saw themselves as developing a "cosmic constitutionalism," in Dwight Waldo's words.

45 Newell, *Tyranny: A New Interpretation*, 508. (Emphasis in the original.) As I understand Nietzsche and Heidegger, they located the first world-transformative instance of the Will to Power in Socrates/Plato, who rebelled against, or resented, the transience of the temporal world. The doctrine of the Ideas prioritized being over becoming. But Heidegger argued that by tyrannically imposing the rule of these otherworldly eternal forms, man was robbed of authentic life in the present; we live only on the earth, in the fleeting here and now. In his 1967 essay "Who is Nietzsche's Zarathustra" in *The Review of Metaphysics*, Heidegger seems to criticize this act of "profound revenge." The effect of the "eternal Ideals as the absolute" is that the "temporal must degrade itself to actual non-being." But "how is man to assume dominion over the earth" if he thus "degrades the earthly"? To save man's properly temporal life, this "spirit of revenge must first vanish. That is why deliverance from the spirit of revenge is the bridge to the highest hope for Zarathustra." For Heidegger, the tyranny of a philosophic *techne* had already occurred when the Ideas became the new cosmopolitan religion of the West. Heidegger seems to reject consciously what the companion in the *Minos* cannot grasp: Socrates's claim that law or *nomos* can only "*wish* to be the discovery of being." The companion, like most humans, wants to equate his regime's account of nature or the whole with what, in fact, *is*. Socrates's odd definition, which may be another way of expressing the doctrine of the separate Ideas, suggests there is always a disconnect or an imperfect match (*chorismos*) between what is and what is *for us*. For Heidegger, it is precisely this act of separating being from life that renders man homeless in the world. His *Dasein* would close the gap, just as the companion in the *Minos* wants to do, between the deeper understanding of *nomos* and what is.

One might see Strauss's remarks at the end of his essay, "What is Liberal Education" as a response to Heidegger's claims. Strauss there describes "the understanding of understanding, by *noesis noeseos*" as "so high, so pure, so noble an experience that Aristotle could ascribe it to his God." When we become "aware of the dignity of the mind, we realize the true ground of the dignity of man and therewith the goodness of the world, whether we understand it as created or as uncreated, which is the home of man because it is the home of the human mind." Strauss, *Liberalism Ancient and Modern*, 8. Consider also his 1954 statement to Alexandre Kojève: "On the basis of the classical presupposition, philosophy requires a radical detachment from human concerns: man must not be absolutely at home on earth, he must be a citizen of the whole." Strauss notes that he and Kojève "both apparently turned away from Being" to address the problem of tyranny, and he seems to be alluding to Heidegger's Nazism when he says, "we have seen that those who lacked the courage to face the issue of Tyranny... were forced to evade the issue of Being as well, precisely because they did nothing but talk of Being." Strauss, *On Tyranny*, 213.

Could one say that from Strauss's perspective Heidegger saw poetry as bringing together man and being, but his neglect of political philosophy meant he did not appreciate the priority of *nomos* in combining and separating what is and what is for us?

46 Neumann, "Is Philosophy Still Possible?" *The Thomist*, October 1972. The subject matter of this book is difficult to discuss precisely because the United States, and the West, are in a period of transition. Neumann's observation in 1972, regarding *traditional* piety versus modern liberal education, is still true in some sense today. But elite opinion has become schizophrenic, embracing both scientific, open-minded tolerance as well as a strident orthodoxy of antiracism. Thus, a twenty-two-year-old in America today might well argue that he is inundated with *nothing but* pronouncements of official piety, while genuinely "humanistic or scientific education" has been reduced to a mere slogan, or rejected outright. My analysis therefore has the added difficulty of trying to capture a moving target.

CHAPTER III

1 "City-state" is the common, if inadequate, English rendition of the Greek word *polis*. See Jaffa's interpretative essay on Aristotle's *Politics* for a treatment of this issue, *The Conditions of Freedom*, 10–14.

2 Fustel de Coulanges, *The Ancient City: A Study on the Religion, Laws, and Institutions of Greece and Rome*, trans. Willard Small, 220, 221.

3 Ibid, 259.

4 Ibid, 271.

5 Ibid, 274–75.

6 See Heidegger's treatment of this "homesickness" in his 1961 Messkirch Centennial: "Everyone is familiar with the phenomena of technological production. We look at them with astonishment. And yet no one knows what in truth this thing is by which man today is being provoked in increasing degree to such boundless activity. What overpowers man in this way can itself be no mere human product. For that reason it remains puzzling and awesome (unheimlich). Yet it is precisely this Awesome that dominates the alien and that through the alien comes towards man, determining his future." The question is whether this homesickness or alienation derives from classical political philosophy or the from the *rejection* of classical political philosophy.

7 Strauss, *Natural Right and History*, 178.

8 Marini, correspondence with the author.

9 Strauss, *What is Political Philosophy?*, 26.

10 See especially *The Political Theory of the American Founding*.

11 Jaffa, *Crisis of the Strauss Divided*, 142. On Jaffa's argument about the compatibility of Aristotle and Locke (sometimes derided as a chimerical "Lockistotle"), consider this statement by Strauss: "The standards for judging political things are inherent in political things as political things for this very reason... and it suffices to think of the difference between Aristotle and Locke regarding the purpose of civil society or of the Commonwealth. But that on which Aristotle and Locke agree is very frequently sufficient for political judgment. We do not always have to raise the most fundamental questions; We can remain sometimes in a more limited horizon. Judgments in this sphere are solid enough...." Quoted in Catherine Zuckert, ed., *Leo Strauss on Political Philosophy: Responding to the Challenges of Positivism and Historicism*, 77.

12 West, "Defending Socrates and Defending Politics: A Response to Stewart Umphrey," *Interpretation*, September 1983.

13 Foucault, *Power/Knowledge*, 93–94.

14 Paul Rabinow, ed., *The Foucault Reader,* 309.

15 Ibid, 315.

16 "Let us read the clearest passage of Marx on the natural root of the division of labor: 'With the development of property the division of labor develops. The division of labor was originally nothing except the division of labor in the sexual act.' Period. In other words – that is of course an absolutely fantastic assertion, because if you want to be

realistic you would have to say that this division of labor is not limited to the sexual act; it has to do with procreation as a whole. You know that men do not become pregnant but women do. But this wholly unreasonable limitation to the sexual act instead of taking the whole, procreation, is characteristic of the whole procedure. Now if you think this through, what is the conclusion? If the division of labor is rooted ultimately in the bisexuality of man – that is the primary form – and the division of labor is to be overcome, let's get rid of the bisexuality. Yet don't laugh…. How can there be a humanism if there is no relevant essential difference between men and brutes, and therefore if there is no relevant essence of man?"

Leo Strauss, seminar on Karl Marx, session 9, April 27, 1960.

Without a definite understanding of the human at its foundation, there can be no law.

17 Schmitt explains the "state of exception" in chapter one of *Political Theology*.

18 *Foucault Reader*, 265–266.

19 It is worth recalling that much of Foucault's early work focused on madness, crime, and sexual deviancy. All societies had regarded certain behaviors as abhorrent, but only within the rational state do structures emerge to manage or regulate all social and political conduct for a comprehensive public good. Foucault was particularly interested in how the definitions of aberrant or deplorable behavior can be extremely fluid, depending on what standard of normalcy the power structure might require. Thus, behavior that might have been regarded as deviant yesterday could be redefined as commendable tomorrow.

20 Foucault, *Power/Knowledge*, 8–9.

21 Rainer Friedrich, "The Enlightenment Gone Mad (II): The Dismal Discourse of Postmodernism's Grand Narratives," *Arion*, 2012.

22 Marini, correspondence with the author.

23 O'Toole, "The Implications for Democracy in a Networked Bureaucratic World," *Journal of Public Administration Research and Theory*, July 1997.

24 Arendt, *New York Review of Books*, February 27, 1969.

25 Terry, "The Thinning of Administration Institutions in the Hollow State," *Administration & Society*, September 2005.

26 Marini, correspondence with the author. This observation was made

just a few weeks before a Pfizer executive was recorded discussing how the company could purposely engineer virus mutations to develop new vaccines. https://mynbc15.com/news/nation-world/undercover-video-allegedly-shows-pfizer-exec-suspects-covid-resulted-from-virus-mutations-in-wuhan-coronavirus-jordon-trishton-walker-project-veritas

27 Sementelli, "Authority, Domination, and the Administrative State," *Administrative Theory & Praxis*, March 2007.

28 "Darius, during his own rule, called together some of the Greeks who were in attendance on him and asked them what would they take to eat their dead fathers. They said that no price in the world would make them do so. After that Darius summoned those of the Indians who are called Callatians, who do eat their parents, and, in the presence of the Greeks (who understood the conversation through an interpreter), asked them what price would make them burn their dead fathers with fire. They shouted aloud, 'Don't mention such horrors!' These are matters of settled custom, and I think Pindar is right when he says, 'Custom is king of all.'" Herodotus, *History*, 3.38, trans. David Grene.

29 Seminar on the *Republic*, session 10, May 2, 1957.

30 Ibid, session 11, May 7.

31 It is unclear to me how those Straussians who at least suggest that nihilism is the terrible truth take Strauss, or philosophy, or anything else seriously. If we can have no knowledge of nature, and the cosmos is simply flux, it seems impossible to defend any logos at all. Isn't this literally the misology which, according to the *Phaedo*, is the worst thing?

32 Many, though not all, Straussians accept that at some level, philosophy too requires an act of faith. Probably the most ambitious attempt to argue that Strauss disproved revelation and rationally demonstrated the validity of philosophy is Heinrich Meier's *Leo Strauss and the Theologico-Political Problem*. Somewhere between Foucault's rejection of reason and a complete science of the human things one might make the eccentric suggestion that the man's place in the whole is not absurd, but it is ironic.

33 "*Omnes et Singulatim: Towards a Criticism of Political Reason*," Tanner Lectures on Human Values, 1979.

34 Rosen, *Hermeneutics as Politics*, 190.

CHAPTER IV

1   Foucault said in his last interview, "My whole philosophical development has been determined by my reading of Heidegger." Quoted in Babette Babich, "'A Philosophical Shock': Foucault's Reading of Heidegger and Nietzsche," *Foucault's Legacy*.

2   Strauss, *What is Political Philosophy?*, 80.

3   Strauss, *Persecution and the Art of Writing*, 155. Consider the comment by Thomas West, noted above, regarding those Straussians who seem unable to understand political life except through texts.

4   Strauss, *City and Man*, 240.

5   Zentner, "The Philosopher and the City: Harry Jaffa and the Straussians," *Interpretation*, Summer 2003.

6   Neumann, *Liberalism*, 53.

7   Agamben, *Where Are We Now*, 97.

8   Strauss, *Natural Right and History*, 32.

9   Jill Abramson, the former executive editor of the *New York Times*, declared in a March 7, 2018, article for *The Guardian*, "It's easy to look at what's happening in Washington DC and despair. That's why I carry a little plastic Obama doll in my purse. I pull him out every now and then to remind myself that the United States had a progressive, African American president until very recently."

10 Strauss, *The Rebirth of Classical Political Rationalism*, 43–44.

11 Marini, "After Trump: The Political and Moral Legitimacy of American Government," *The American Mind*, October 23, 2018.

12 See Mattias Desmet's *The Psychology of Totalitarianism* for an analysis of how modern science has become an ideology that induces "mass formation" hypnosis.

13 Catherine Zuckert, ed., *Leo Strauss on Political Philosophy: Responding to the Challenge of Positivism and Historicism*, 123.

14 Jaffa, *American Conservatism and the American Founding*, 155.

15 Strauss, *What is Political Philosophy?*, 130.

16 Strauss, *On Tyranny*, 275.

A NOTE ON THE TYPE

THE NARROW PASSAGE *has been set in in Jonathan Hoefler's Mercury types. Originally created for the* New Times *newspaper chain and later adapted for general informational typography, the Mercury types were drawn in four grades intended to be used under variable printing conditions – that is, to compensate for less-than-optimal presswork or for regional differences in paper stock and plant conditions. The result was a family of types that were optimized to print well in a vast number of sizes and formats. In books, Mercury makes a no-nonsense impression, crisp and open, direct and highly readable, yet possessed of real style and personality.*

DESIGN & COMPOSIITON BY CARL W. SCARBROUGH